(1998)

Touched by Fire

ALSO BY ELLIOTT LEYTON

The Compact (ed.)

The One Blood

Bureaucracy and World View (with Don Handelman)

Violence and Public Anxiety
(with William O'Grady and James Overton)

Serial Murder (ed.)

Dying Hard

The Myth of Delinquency

Hunting Humans

Sole Survivor

Men of Blood

TOUCHED BY FIRE

*Doctors Without Borders
in a Third World Crisis*

Elliott Leyton

Photographs by Greg Locke

M&S

Canadian Cataloguing in Publication Data

Leyton, Elliott, 1939-
      Touched by fire : Doctors Without Borders in a third world crisis

Includes bibliographical references and index.
ISBN 0-7710-5305-3

1. Doctors Without Borders (Association).   2. Genocide – Rwanda – History – 20th century.   3. Rwanda – History – Civil War, 1994 – Medical care.   I. Locke, Greg.   II. Title.

DT450.435.L49 1998   967.57104   C98-930203-2

We acknowledge the financial support of the Government of Canada through the Book Publishing Industry Development Program for our publishing activities. We further acknowledge the support of the Canada Council for the Arts and the Ontario Arts Council for our publishing program.

Set in Plantin by M&S, Toronto
Printed and bound in Canada

McClelland & Stewart Inc.
The Canadian Publishers
481 University Avenue
Toronto, Ontario
M5G 2E9

1 2 3 4 5 6   03 02 91 00 99 98

Contents

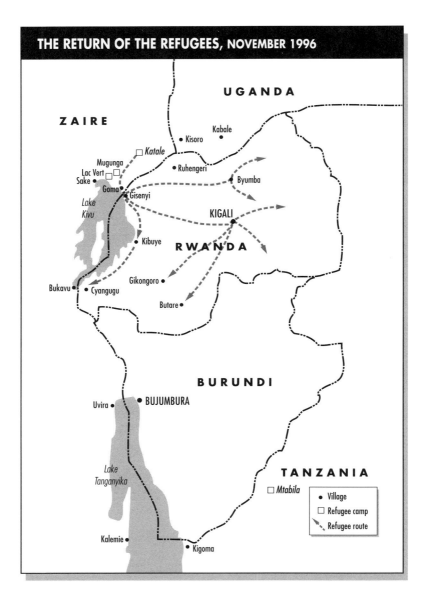

THE RETURN OF THE REFUGEES, NOVEMBER 1996

UGANDA

ZAIRE

• Kisoro   Kabale •

☐ *Katale*

Mugunga
Lac Vert
Sake •   ☐☐
Goma •   • Gisenyi   Byumba •

• Ruhengeri

Lake Kivu

KIGALI

• Kibuye   RWANDA

Bukavu •   • Cyangugu   Gikongoro •

Butare •

BURUNDI

Uvira •   • BUJUMBURA

Lake Tanganyika

TANZANIA

☐ *Mtabila*

• Village
☐ Refugee camp
Refugee route

Kalemie •   • Kigoma

Preface

Why do the front-line medical, nursing, and support personnel in international aid agencies take such astonishing personal risks in their emergency work in the Third World? Do humanitarian organizations deserve the billions of dollars they receive each year from the industrialized world? Does this vast expenditure offer any significant return, either to the intended beneficiaries or to the donors? As the first sustained "inside" look at the humanitarian industry's most illustrious emergency medical teams – Doctors Without Borders – this book struggles to answer these questions.

The idea for this volume – and the art exhibit that both parallels and complements it – germinated during idle conversations between a photographer, an anthropologist, and an artist. Each brought to the discussions a distinctive background and perspective: Greg Locke, a seasoned international photo-journalist at ease in the Third World; Elliott Leyton, an academic specialist in human aggression; and Bonnie Leyton, a well-known Newfoundland artist.

Our proposal to examine the motivations, dilemmas, risks, and achievements of these emergency medical teams did not become reality until we were given the status of unpaid temporary staff members with Doctors Without Borders (better known to the rest of the world as Médecins Sans Frontières or, more simply, MSF). In the process, we became a small part of the effort that was about to be launched to meet Rwanda's post-genocidal refugee crisis. We arrived in Rwanda in November 1996 just as the murderous Interhamwe militia, licking its wounds in neighbouring Zaire after its resounding defeat in 1994–95, fell back under increased military pressure from the Rwandan government and its Zairean allies and allowed hundreds of thousands of displaced Rwandans from the separate Tutsi and Hutu diasporas to flood back into Rwanda. Simultaneously, Zaire – which had given shelter to so many Interhamwe killers and warlords – descended even further into anarchy and eventual collapse.

This was a potentially dangerous situation for everyone, but we were very lucky. We left Rwanda with only a hand grenade thrown as a "warning" into the garden behind our tent in Gisenyi ("an *avertissement*," said the French radio operator, Balzac, signalling with characteristic foresight the brutality that was to come); an ignored body of a dead boy on the road below the MSF team's house; and heavy anti-aircraft fire at the circling American reconnaissance airplane overhead. Locke endured more than our simple anxiety: he walked twenty kilometres through the baking Zairean countryside in one day to find and follow MSF workers; and he contracted malaria in the flooded and mosquito-infested refugee camps on the Somalia–Kenya border.

Yet it was only weeks after we left Rwanda that Interhamwe death squads – having tried but failed to breach the gates of our MSF house – burst into an adjacent medical compound and murdered three unarmed Spanish Médicos del Mundo medical workers and three Rwandan soldiers, as well as dozens of civilians. Many more Interhamwe massacres of Tutsi refugees, clergy, and children were to follow – with Tutsi children being separated from their Hutu schoolmates and then shot dead in the classroom.

Even before this trip, Bonnie Leyton and Greg Locke shared the modern and civilized sensibility that an encounter with other societies is inherently enriching and ennobling – even intoxicating. This was never the case with Elliott Leyton, who insisted that exotic travel was merely a dumb rehearsal and reprise of the imperial spirit, and the humanitarian industry was a kind of glamorous make-work scheme for the First World's middle classes. We all had much to learn from one another in that autumn of 1996 as we orbited through Central Africa in our claustrophobic MSF capsule.

One of the many things that held us together was our admiration for what would be the model for this book – John Berger and Jean Mohr's *A Seventh Man*, a symphony of text and photographs that we emulated in this bloodier locale. We wish therefore to emphasize that this book is the product of a full and equal partnership between Leyton and Locke, writer and photographer. The photographs are not intended simply to illustrate the text; rather, they tell their own story. Neither is the text designed to provide mere extended captions for the photographs. Each struggles to construct his own meaningful narrative – parallel but separate and distinct discourses – out of a series of observations, conversations, and scenes absorbed during our participation in the frantic and crisis-driven world of MSF.[1]

No one who works with MSF survives the experience emotionally or financially unscathed. Elliott Leyton is therefore especially grateful (as is Greg Locke) to McClelland & Stewart, his Canadian publishers for a quarter-century – notably Douglas Gibson and Jonathan Webb – not only for the grave concerns they expressed about our safety, but also for the advance that was offered when our finances were in their most perilous state. In addition, Memorial University's Office of Research awarded Elliott Leyton a grant from its Social Sciences and Humanities Research Council fund; while Terrence Murphy, Ronald Schwartz, and Ben Chapman offered many kindnesses. Both Greg Locke and Bonnie Leyton wish to acknowledge the assistance of Ann Anderson, the Canada/Newfoundland Agreement on Economic Renewal, and the Newfoundland and Labrador Arts Council. Locke also wishes to thank Sue Hammond, Ann Locke, and Fred Locke.

Most of all, we are indebted to on-the-ground MSF personnel in Kenya, Canada, Rwanda, Somalia, Zaire, and the Netherlands. It is true that the mentality of many MSF press officers and bureaucrats seemed indistinguishable from their cynical and manipulative counterparts in any bureaucratic sector – whether corporate, government, media, or university. Yet the medical workers and support staff in the field were the most splendid group of big-hearted and monomaniacal, introverted and sanctimonious, cosmopolitan and disputatious, socially awkward and self-critical, dogmatic and courageous characters we have ever encountered. It would be invidious to single out individuals by name, and tedious to list them all, but they surely know who they are.

The War, the Famine, the Flood, the Plague

> *"The grave is only half full.*
> *Who will help us fill it?"*
> *– Rwandan government radio, April 1994*[2]

"The grave is not yet full," the Rwandan government radio proclaimed. "Kill them all." Radio is the only means of mass communication in an impoverished African nation, and the Nazis taught us long ago that to control the national radio is to control the people. The Nazis also taught us – if such a lesson needed to be learned – that the human reluctance to kill is rarely extended to other ethnic groups. We should be grateful to the Nazis because they taught us so much.

In neighbouring Burundi a quarter-century before, the oppressive ruling Tutsis had ruthlessly murdered 250,000 "influential" Hutus. Now in Rwanda, the Hutus were the

Opposite: Hutu refugees on the road to Rwanda, November 1996.

oppressors, and the radio said clearly what the loyal Hutus must do. They must kill all the Tutsis: "Kill them all. Spare none, or their children will return to kill us." They must also "kill all those Hutus who will not help us in this sacred duty of the Interhamwe militia – we who fight together." The people did what they were told, and did so with varying degrees of enthusiasm. Months later, when their side was defeated in one of the most daring military manoeuvres of our century, the *genocidaires* claimed they murdered their neighbours only out of fear that they themselves would be killed. But no examples could be found of the punishment of any reluctantly homicidal Hutu.

There had not been enough guns to go around, and in any case bullets were deemed too expensive for the likes of Tutsis: the ubiquitous flat-bladed machetes (pangas), or any farm or kitchen implement, would do the job just as well. Thus the Rwandan tragedy became one of the few genocides in our century to be accomplished almost entirely without firearms. Indeed, it took many strong and eager arms to carry out the strenuous work of raping, burning, and hacking to death a half-million people (and mutilating many thousands more by slicing off their hands, their breasts, their genitals, or their ears) with pangas, kitchen knives, farm hoes, pitchforks, and hastily improvised spiked clubs.

The killings went on for one hundred nightmare days in that spring of 1994. Children, women, and men sought in vain for sanctuary in their homes, in the churches, fields, and schools; and only a few escaped capture when they hid. Soon most of the Tutsi population of Rwanda would be annihilated. Their remains would be left to rot where they fell, or were dumped in the nearest river. For months the rivers of Rwanda would vomit bloated and mutilated corpses, just as other bodies choked the wells, fields and churches, city streets and villages. "The grave is not yet full." The active volcanoes of Rwanda glowed. The people spoke in whispers of "rape houses," where young women would be kept to be abused, tortured, and murdered.

Seventeen months later in Kigali, an inconsolable Dutch journalist told how he had numbly watched the catastrophe unfold. He had heard the screams on the streets and helplessly watched the pangas sink deep into living flesh. Finally, he chose a menial penitential task, offering a form of decent burial to the victims still oozing fresh blood – he rolled their bodies in bamboo carpets, covering himself in the ever-flowing blood of Rwanda. "Who will help us fill the grave?" He was a journalist, not a humanitarian agency's nurse or doctor, and he was working with the still-twitching freshly dead, not the living. He gagged as he recalled his profane form of divine sacrifice. His declaration of independence from our barbarous past and present is a metaphor for the seemingly pointless human acts that alone can save this planet from deserving self-immolation. It cannot be otherwise, for too many everywhere are ready to help fill the graves.

ᔕ

It is a stunning experience to sit as we did in the garden of a gracious home overlooking the countless misty green hills of Kigali and imagine the stinking, sweating desperate fear in that household on the night the Interhamwe came with their machetes to rid the world of this Tutsi rubbish. They would easily have breached the stone walls and high hedges that surrounded the house and provided an illusion of protection – and it was nothing more than illusion, since the government had forbidden private ownership of firearms. That was how we now shivered in the cool November night air, seventeen months after what the Tutsis matter-of-factly call "the genocide." We were naïvely armed only with our notebooks, our cameras, and our good intentions; but it was not difficult to picture the shrieking slow and liquid death for all in the house. The Interhamwe had come months before we arrived in that hillside house, but they would brush near us many more times, when they would shoot into crowds of refugees or schoolchildren, or execute aid workers who had become convenient targets and embarrassing "witnesses."

Later that same night on a Kigali hilltop, in one of the few reopened restaurants in the city, we downed a plate of pasta and a glass of mediocre wine from the bar's denuded stock – acquired months after the One Hundred Days of Massacre, when the killers had snaked across the restaurant's open lawn and used their reddened axes and pangas to obliterate all those who toiled within. Yet Le Cactus Pizza was now no different from any tropical outdoor restaurant, except that most of the vehicles parked outside were plastered with the logos of the two hundred international aid agencies competing for the advertising opportunities made available to them by the Rwandan catastrophe. The impeccably dressed clientele could have been found in any fashionable watering hole from New York to Paris, apparently oblivious to their surroundings. Certainly the braying and demanding upper-class voices of the press officers, journalists, and international aid bureaucrats who had seen it all blurred seamlessly with all the indifference on the planet. Nevertheless, the voice of one MSF press officer pierced the air. Explaining to a journalist how difficult it was for someone as aristocratic as herself to work with "natives," she said, "I just can't relate to some peasant who lives in a hut and shits on the road."

Rwanda Remembers:
"I Only Cut Off Your Brother's Hands"

At the height of the Rwandan holocaust, Sam Gody hid to escape the fate of his six brothers and sisters. Seventeen months later, after the return of the refugees in the autumn of 1996, Sam confronted the destroyer of his family – Innocent Nsengiyumva, a farmer he had known for years. "He had a normal face," Sam said. "He never said sorry or expressed remorse. I became shy when I saw him. I couldn't understand what happened. First, I greeted him. Then I said, 'Is it true you killed my family?'" "I only cut off your brother's hands," Innocent explained, exonerating himself in this fashion for a small offence. "Others came and killed him," he claimed. Not I, not I, he suggested, making what seemed to him to be reasonable recompense by naming the "others," the guilty ones.

Genocidaire Innocent told distinguished journalist Alan Zarembo how he was able to beat two children to death with a club. "I didn't want to. I didn't mean to kill them. I didn't know what I was doing. If you were there, things were strange. I can't find a way to explain it to you. Can you imagine the radio saying, 'Go kill these people'?"

He has a point. Government orders had instantly organized the infinitely hierarchical Hutu world, in which each cluster of ten houses had a leader who was connected to all other local group leaders in the commune, themselves under the direction of regional authorities who in turn received their instructions by radio from the central government. "The message got to the local authorities," Innocent explained. "They mobilized the soldiers and the militias, and they were going to the villages getting civilians to kill people. We accepted. They said we were fighting for the country."

Innocent seems to have truly loved fighting for his country and may well have been responsible for many more murders than the two child killings to which he admits. How could he help but enjoy the massacre when it was all done in such a communal carnival spirit, and with such encouragement and approval from the central authorities?

In our imagination, only those trained to blind obedience or fanaticism can be capable of such atrocities: but here, it was clearly *fun*. "Whenever we passed a bar, we drank. Sometimes we bought it, sometimes the soldiers stole it. We used to go back to our houses for lunch. After lunch, we got together again." And it was all done so economically: the soldiers told them to use machetes and clubs on the unarmed Tutsis, not to waste bullets on the likes of them. It helped, too, to *personalize* the experience, to feel the living flesh of their arrogant former rulers yield to their blows.

At first, Innocent told Zarembo, he had found himself unable to take part and had merely watched others do the killings, "like a child watching something his father is doing." But he soon fell into the spirit of the occasion, and when he saw the two Tutsi children who stood there frozen in fear, he drove his nail-studded club into their heads. "I didn't run to them. I didn't call them. They were just there and I killed them. There were so many people there."[3]

The Meaning of Genocide: "Who Cares About a Bunch of Niggers?"

On what seems to be another planet, a rough-edged Quebec businessman asks me: "Why bother, anyway? Who cares about a bunch of niggers? They made their own problems. *Let* them finish each other off if that's what they want!" In a similar spirit, in a warm Ontario living room, a smiling, elderly white woman gives breath to a widespread sentiment when she says, "It's impossible to bring Africa into the twentieth century. People have been trying for *ages*." Have they indeed? This is primitive Africa, after all, the continent we despise the most, fertile soil for genocides. Even the occasional renegade anthropologist will confirm our suspicions about such places, teach us to expect nothing but catastrophe and blood from such people. Pierre Clastres writes: "Should war cease, the heart of primitive society will cease to beat. War is its foundation, the very life of its being, it is its goal: primitive society is *society for war*, it is, by definition, warlike."[4]

Yet war is not a primitive invention, and genocide is certainly not an African aberration. Genocide has always been with us, but its modern form – politically motivated and rationally planned extermination within a society – is a largely European invention. Moreover, that invention is the essence of modernity. Genocide as political strategy is *the* story of the twentieth century, when whole peoples have been flushed down the toilet of history, "disappeared" to ensure mass obedience and to advance the petty ambitions of their ruling elites. What simpler way can there be for a modern state to galvanize its citizens, divert public attention from the regime's defects, steal the victims' wealth and status, and terrorize the survivors into submission than to perpetrate mass rape and annihilation on a defenceless minority?

How else can we begin to understand the Nazi extermination of the Jews and Gypsies, or the Khmer Rouge desecration of the Cambodian "bourgeoisie"? We steal their lives and their land, and in this dishonour bind together our nation and enrich both our rulers and ourselves. For historian Arnold Toynbee, what distinguishes twentieth-century genocide from the horrors that precede it is that it is "committed in cold-blood by the deliberate *fiat* of holders of despotic political power, and that the perpetrators of genocide employ all the resources of present-day technology and organization to make their planned massacres systematic and complete."[5]

One of the most perceptive sociologists of our time, Zygmunt Bauman, reiterates that genocide is a quintessentially modern form of "social engineering," a plan that requires a "rational, bureaucratically organized power" to fulfil. Modern genocide is genocide with a specific purpose: "getting rid of the adversary is not an end in itself," it is merely the means to an end – "a grand vision of a better, and radically different, society." In this grand vision, a "perfect society" will be possible only when it is freed of the cancerous encumbrances of Tutsis, Gypsies, capitalists, communists, homosexuals, or Jews.[6]

The modern routine deployment of genocide as a tactical option for the political convenience of the nation-state began in Turkey. At the close of the nineteenth century, the crumbling Ottoman Empire was surrounded by the rapacious European nations anxious to loot the ancient Empire's vast domain. Casting about for a solution to their problems, the Turkish rulers proposed this clever way to deal simultaneously with the occasionally rebellious Armenians and to find a public scapegoat for their growing internal instability. The pilot project they devised – the massacre of the Armenians in

1895 under the leadership of the Turkish Sultan Abdul-Hamid – became the blueprint for modern genocide. This precocious holocaust was "designed as a sort of ambassadorial note to the European powers to refrain from intervention in the domestic affairs of Turkey, and a most bloody warning to the Armenians themselves against [destabilizing the Empire by] seeking the intercession of these powers on their behalf or aspiring to autonomy." [7]

It took another twenty years to perfect and routinize this modern architecture of mass death. In 1915, the Turkish government uncoiled its plan to eliminate entirely the Armenian presence in Turkey. Accused *en masse* of treason by the Empire's rulers, most of Turkey's one million Armenians were rounded up for deportation and forced to begin a long winter's march through the mountains to Syria. The Muslim society's traditional antipathy towards the Christian (and commercially successful) Armenians was manipulated by the government until the ensuing mass "slaughter had some appearance of spontaneous action by mobs of Turkish peasants and townsmen and massacring bands of Kurds and Circassians." The religious prejudice only added to the ferocity, and "terrible atrocities against priests" were especially notable. Without food, water, or proper clothing, the Armenians were kidnapped, robbed, harassed, raped, and murdered by the local populace, and shot if they faltered by the Turkish soldiers. The starvation, exhaustion, assault, and thirst that inevitably followed ensured that only a handful of Armenians survived this tramp into eternity. [8]

To this day, the Turkish government refuses to accept responsibility for (or even acknowledge) this mother of modern genocides. Nevertheless, its remarkable political experiment was studied with great interest around the world, both by dictators seeking mechanisms to strengthen their own regimes (as with Stalin, Pol Pot, or Hitler) and by ruling elites anxious to reinforce their stranglehold on their own public (as in Argentina or El Salvador). These twentieth-century social techniques would now be commonly deployed against marginal members of almost any state. Indeed, the tactic of genocide would be taken up and refined by Germany, the Soviet Union, Cambodia, Rwanda, Burundi, Uganda, India, Pakistan, Yugoslavia, Brazil, Guatemala, Paraguay, Nigeria, Indonesia, Liberia, and China, among many others. It has stolen one hundred million lives or more in our century. No one understood its utility as a political tactic more cynically than Hitler, who early in his career made perfectly clear the planned and "logical" character of his racist theme: "Anti-Semitism is a *useful revolutionary expedient*. Anti-Semitic propaganda in all countries is an almost indispensable medium in the extension of our political campaign. You will see how little time we shall need in order to upset the ideas and criteria of the whole world simply and solely by attacking Judaism. It is beyond question the most important weapon in our propaganda arsenal."[9]

Genocide is not of course "exclusively a crime of governments," although racist violence is perhaps the essence of twentieth-century statecraft. Obviously, too, genocide is not necessarily part of "the strategies and goals of elites" in every nation-state. Moreover, in many nations whose governments have not declared a genocide, "entrepreneurial" individuals and groups have eagerly assisted in such matters on their own and for their own purposes, as in Poland, the Ukraine, France, Israel, and Palestine. But its effectiveness is now widely appreciated by ruthless politicians, and it lurks as a potential weapon in every modern national armoury – useful in either a struggle for power between lawless "contending elites" or to consolidate dictatorial power in a "scapegoat genocidal massacre." In theory, at least, unless overpowered by robust democratic institutions, a genocide can now be orchestrated anywhere and at any time.[10]

Even when no genocide is intended, in modern war it is civilians, not opposing troops, who are the primary "military" targets, accounting for an estimated 74 per cent of all casualties in wars in the 1980s (in the nineteenth century, European civilians of course also died in war, but only if they happened to be in the way). In Central African wars, it is even worse: the casualties are virtually all civilians – and so they should be, since civilians cannot shoot back and are thus quite safe to rape, loot, and kill. Better still, civilians are the soft but strong shield behind which modern armies can hide (whether in Beirut, Chechnya, Croatia, or Zaire) and thus assure their own safety. In Zaire throughout 1996 and 1997, both the Hutu militia and the Tutsi allies kidnapped and killed at will, preying on "the enemy's" defenceless civilians.[11]

Rwandan History

Yet how could it have happened in Rwanda? Surely not in the midst of such stunning beauty, with its endless conical hills wrapped in emerald green and its enormous, placid blue lakes? It is not even "naturally" poor: it may be one of the smallest and most densely populated countries in the world, but its rich soil and abundant rainfall have ensured that only man-made catastrophes can cause a famine in Rwanda.

Journalist Fergal Keane, in his remarkable *Season of Blood*, reminds us that Tutsis and Hutus have not always been locked in a death struggle. If for centuries the Tutsis formed the aristocracy and the Hutus were essentially exploited medieval serfs, Rwanda was a relatively open social hierarchy – Hutus who became wealthy enough to purchase their own cattle were "assimilated" into the aristocracy and took on a Tutsi identity. An ugly fault line in Tutsi culture, however, was the assumption that their "tallness and aquiline facial features were synonymous with superiority." Historian Gerard Prunier reminds us that the "most respected anthropologists of the time" rushed to develop this dangerous set of racist ideas; and, as MSF intellectuals note, the prejudice played into the hands of the German and Belgian empires that seized Rwanda for exploitation. These European colonials, besotted with the bogus racial theories, further refined the doctrines. Thus, the Hutus came to be seen as flat-nosed and thick-lipped "negroids," "childish in nature, both timid and lazy," and, of course, "extremely dirty"; while the Tutsis were "reserved, courteous and elegant," and possessed of an "air of refinement." The colonials recognized at once that the Tutsis were fit to serve as their political puppets, Keane notes, a social class that "could be trusted to carry out the orders of the white men." [12]

Still, the system remained slightly permeable – with successful Hutus "becoming" Tutsis – until 1933, when the Belgians foreshadowed apartheid by introducing to the colony a system of mandatory identity cards tagged with name and ethnicity. In doing so, ethnic identity was fixed for all time. The possession of a few cows could no longer transform a lowly Hutu into an aristocratic Tutsi; now the Hutu truly became feudal serfs, corralled through forced labour to "serve in perpetuity" their exploitative Tutsi overlords. Naturally, this sealing of the social divide intensified antagonisms between the solidified ethnic groups, as did the brutal suppression of Hutu aspirations.

To further destabilize the situation, when independence from Belgium approached during the 1950s, the Belgians – seeing that the minority Tutsis would be vanquished in any one-man-one-vote system – switched sides. When the old Tutsi king died in 1959 and the Hutus rebelled, "the Belgians did little or nothing to save the lives of the besieged Tutsis." Somewhere between ten thousand and one hundred thousand Tutsis were massacred. Philosopher Bertrand Russell understood at the time that this was the "most horrible and systematic human massacre we have had occasion to witness since the extermination of the Jews by the Nazis." Tens of thousands of Tutsis fled into exile in Tanzania, Uganda, and elsewhere, to form the Tutsi diaspora.

In Rwanda, a corrupt new government operated on behalf of the revitalized Hutu elites. Fergal Keane notes that it "siphoned off vast sums in public funds and turned the civil service into a party jobs machine." It also led the way in propagating racist attitudes, fears, and assaults. An additional ten thousand Tutsis were murdered in one pogrom alone in 1963. This was followed by another major massacre of Tutsis in 1967, and consolidated in the early 1970s with a political campaign designed "to drive the [Tutsi] minority from all of the country's educational institutions."

The army of the Tutsi diaspora – the Rwandan Patriotic Front (RPF) – learned its trade in exile while it served with the forces that ultimately overthrew Uganda's murderous dictator, Idi Amin. In 1990, the RPF began its offensive in Rwanda. The Rwandan government, aware of the economic havoc wreaked throughout the country by its corruption, responded in modern fashion by playing the genocidal card. It began with what Keane called a renewal of the "scapegoating" of Tutsis: rather than relinquish power to the opposition headed by a coalition of Tutsis and Hutu moderates, the regime would "drag the old bogey out of the closet and direct the anger of the poor in the direction of the Tutsis." It would resurrect genocide on a grander scale, using government radio to disseminate its propaganda and to organize the killers through the Hutu hierarchy of commune, village, and hamlet. In this way, the elites proceeded immediately to mobilize the militia, regional and village leaders, as well as the common people, to begin the genocide.

During the infamous One Hundred Days of Massacre, Keane records, "up to one million people were hacked, shot, strangled, clubbed and burned to death," and many more were "wounded, raped and terrorized." The international community stood by and did nothing. The United Nations (UN) prevaricated and provided only a worthless token military force with neither power, personnel, nor equipment. Meanwhile, the RPF's military leader, Paul Kagame, manoeuvred and struck deftly with his tiny army until the Hutu army collapsed and fled to Zaire in 1994.[13]

In their flight, the Interhamwe warlords took with them hundreds of thousands of Hutu refugees, whose function would be to serve as both a human shield and a legitimizing constituency for the new warlords of the refugee camps in Zaire. In defeat, but fed by well-meaning UN personnel, the militias began re-arming themselves with weapons eagerly supplied by international arms dealers. As is its custom, the militia preyed upon its own civilians, subjecting them to the usual blackmail, robbery, rape, and murder. Numerous press reports recorded how the Interhamwe assured civilian "loyalty" by staging occasional terror-massacres in the camps, sometimes merely running through the camps firing their weapons randomly into the crowds. The UN reported that at least two hundred thousand refugees had fled still farther, seeking refuge in the forests and "surviving on food found in villages and fields, consisting mostly of tree roots and rotten sweet potatoes." Hundreds were dying each day, sometimes from bullets but more often from dehydration and bloody diarrhea. The *New York Times* marvelled that fear of Interhamwe's diktat was so great that "most of the refugees are moving westward, with little food or water, into some of the most inhospitable terrain in the world, rather than turning homeward" to Rwanda.[14]

In the meantime, the victorious Tutsi diaspora had seized control of Rwanda's government and claimed it wished to create a remodelled non-racist state. It also intensified its military pressure in Zaire until early November 1996, when the Hutu militias lost control of the camps and the refugees flooded back into Rwanda. Overwhelmed Rwandan customs officials opened the border, and the refugees marched across in an unbroken wave, heading to their homes.

Our Story

We had come to spend a month with Doctors Without Borders (Médecins Sans Frontières to most of the world or, simply, MSF) in Rwanda – Greg Locke, the photographer; Elliott Leyton, the writer; and Bonnie Leyton, the artist – and then to follow that with separate visits to other tormented African nations. During that time, we would live as they did, grabbing a slim foam pad or mattress and claiming a floor space wherever we found ourselves for the night, eating a portion of whatever was in the refrigerator – when there was anything at all. At our first African stop, in Kenya, we joined the hundreds of sweating journalists and aid personnel in Nairobi's airport fighting for space on the few airplanes flying into Kigali. Tension mounted at the long lines in front of the airline counters as the once-a-day flight was about to leave. It was then that some network television journalists burdened with mountains of camera equipment and too much money used their "influence" and their bribes to muscle their way onto the plane. "It's time to play hardball," one helpfully explained to all around him. The airplane was so heavily laden it could barely take flight before it reached the end of the runway. We swallowed our fear of what was to come, and watched in amazement as, with racist abandon, the non-African businessmen insulted and tormented the native Kenyan air stewards, demanding beer and a light for their cigarettes before the plane had even left the ground, with flicks of their fingers and shouts of "Instantly!"

We came to record the humanitarian activities of MSF. It was only by chance that the afternoon we arrived in Rwanda – Friday, November 15, 1996 – was the day the Zaire–Rwanda border posts crumbled and the exiles flooded back to their Rwandan homes. When the news came that Friday, we were in the capital city, Kigali, ninety minutes south of the Zaire border. "Bad timing!" Ronald, the irrepressible MSF administrator, told us, "I knew it the moment you arrived." * In this

---

*Throughout this book, I follow MSF custom in referring to MSFers only by their first names.

way he signalled to us that in such an emergency, all the promises MSF had made to our project about drivers, interpreters, and access to personnel would be swept aside without explanation or apology, and we would be on our own. We sat in the fading tropical light in the MSF administrative headquarters, a once-gracious colonial home surrounded by stone and steel walls topped with broken glass, and converted into dozens of offices packed with computers and telephones, Xerox machines and MSF administrators.

"One hundred thousand refugees just crossed the border – it's fantastic!" shouted a voice over the staccato bark of the printers pumping out MSF news bulletins. "The information that we have now," he shouted to anyone who could hear him in the darkened corridors, "is that the border control has completely broken, and people are pouring into Rwanda. . . . Stand by! There's some news coming in. . . . Okay, at the moment they're coming in at six thousand per hour, people are destroying their identity papers." The great return had begun. The innocent and the guilty were coming home, the latter hiding their identities in the hope their victims would not find them.

TIC-TAC
1973 – THE YEAR WE START
TO HAVE A BETTER LIFE.
– Refugee's T-shirt on the road from Zaire

The following morning, we jump into the back of the spartan MSF Toyota Land Cruiser heading north with a cargo of medicine and one Dutch water and sanitation specialist. In this fashion we sprint for the Zairean border, the universal symbol for "no weapons" (a line drawn across a Kalashnikov assault rifle) plastering our doors and windows. We cringe as our Rwandan driver pushes the vehicle too fast – as they all do – ignoring the increasing numbers of refugees clinging to the edge of the winding mountain road. The next day, at high speed along the narrow highway, our car's mirror will clip a child and send his living body spinning into the ditch. When Locke – himself the father of a young daughter – shouts at the indifferent Rwandan driver and soon protests to MSF, a press officer tells him to shut up, that "we're here saving thousands of lives, we can't stop for every traffic accident, and we can't let our best drivers go!" That night, presumably to cover herself, the press officer will file a complaint to MSF about this troublesome and finicky Locke. Meanwhile, on the road to Zaire, unaccustomed to the heat and the attendant problems of dehydration, I am embarrassed to insist that they pull over to the side of the road and allow me to be sick. The relief is only temporary, since I will be gripped by a constant stomach-churning nausea for the next six weeks.

Ominously, four superbly fit military men, thinly disguised as Hutu refugees, run abreast like apocalyptic horses to Kigali.

We spend the night at yet another gracious colonial estate that serves as MSF's local headquarters. Locke heads for Zaire with the keys to Goma's MSF office in his pocket: he does not know that the office is now just a shell, ransacked and

Hutu refugees and Rwandan soldier, Rwanda, 1996.

gutted by looters. Bonnie and I spend the day travelling up the highway in yet another Land Cruiser with an MSF nurse, Monique, a tough and confident Dutch woman whose task is to ensure that all arrangements have been made to treat any illness among the refugees.

As we drive farther north, we reach the first MSF way station (MSF's standard portable tent "hospital") – consisting of an expatriate European nurse with a few "national" Rwandan assistants, a tent for rehydration and recovery, water available from faucets connected to a giant bladder flown in from Europe, and a latrine dug the day before. Only a few hundred refugees have made it this far, wretched, sweat-soaked, and mud-spattered, many of them clothed in the castoffs of Europe – one man without shoes wears a sweatshirt that reads "Oxford University." The daily rains have transformed the ground around the way station into a slimy pool of mud; and the stink of smoke and sickness is everywhere. A woman carries a cooking pot on her head in the African style: strapped to its lid are a few ears of corn and two precious chunks of wood for fuel. Some of the tired refugees claim that they are sick and ask for a ride. The powerfully built and purposeful Monique tells us, "Only those who can't walk at all don't have to walk. A car will come for them." Children beg for food, proffering the universal outstretched palm.

After an hour, we leave the way station and head closer to

the border. The highway fills in with some of the hundreds of thousands fleeing from Zaire. Rwandan culture – Hutu and Tutsi alike – dictates that emotions be held inside, and their faces tell us nothing. As we move up, a single line of refugees becomes two or three abreast, and they gradually spill to choke the road, yielding ever-so-reluctantly to the incessantly blowing horns of the military and aid vehicles. The next way station is jammed with thousands of refugees, some lining up for food (packets of the standard BP5 high-protein biscuit distributed by all the aid agencies), others waiting for truck transport to their distant homes. So that's what it means to be "dressed in rags." Their clothing is tattered and peppered with holes, strips of cloth are falling off, the patches themselves are patched and repatched. Many are barefoot, others are in sandals. One man wears rubber boots shredded open from top to sole, and a "Labatt's Blue" T-shirt.

At the Maiseri MSF way station, the endless flow of expressionless people slows to a halt. Most refugees stop to cook their lunch on the side of the road: many of their faces are plastered with the deforming fungus that is contracted from sleeping unprotected on the jungle floor. Beside them, two large and bilious-green MSF medical tents are in operation, rehydrating those who wait patiently in line. The refugees carry their own plastic sheeting that has been supplied to them in the camps by the UN, food, wood, and the ubiquitous yellow plastic jerrycans filled with water. The omnipresent stench of burning grass and dung is nauseating. The bearded and rumpled, yet intensely focused, Dutch MSF epidemiologist

Water and sanitation specialist, near Ruhengeri, Rwanda.

MSF way station on refugee route.

watches for signs of the dreaded cholera among the refugees –
fever and collapse. In 1994, cholera claimed tens of thousands of lives here. It is impossible not to be in awe of the
women striding silently, rhythmically, relentlessly through the
Rwandan mountains with all their worldly goods on their
heads, a baby on their backs, an infant at their sides, and
heavy jerrycans strapped to their waists.

And suddenly we are at the Zairean border. No wonder
the crisis has captured the attention of the world media – it
is so *televisable*, so media-worthy, the squeezed refugees so
easily absorbed by the mindless and memory-less television
camera. Famous American-network television journalists
and anchorpersons are everywhere, driving here and there in
search of the perfect background for their broadcasts. We had
thought all the refugees were moving on the road, but many
of them are *here* in their many thousands, spread cheek by
jowl in some scene from hell, camped out in the pervading
smoke and stink, emptying their bowels and bladders anywhere and everywhere, for hundreds of metres on either side
of the road. Total gridlock is reached at 2:45 P.M.! Vehicles
can no longer move at all. A stupefyingly claustrophobic jam
of people, cars, more people, buses, trucks, and people. In the
midst of this confusion, a woman takes her two-gallon jerry-
can from her waist, offering it first to the two-year-old on
her knee, who sucks greedily. Only then does she allow herself
some water. Refreshed, she puts down the jug, removes her
breast from under her shirt, and feeds her infant. What was
it that Martin, a veteran MSF M.D., had said to us months

earlier at an MSF conference in Canada? "African women make wonderful mothers."

The chaos continues for several days until the Rwandan government seems to panic. In fact, the government has made a logical military decision, and it is the humanitarian aid agencies that have panicked. The government is legitimately concerned that this sudden release of the refugees may be a clever Interhamwe tactic, designed to clog the roads and strangle any government military response. The Rwandan military decides to close the aid workers' hospitals and rest camps in order to keep the refugees moving. The decision is not sensitively implemented: soldiers drive the relatively healthy out of the hospitals, and carry to the waiting buses those "vulnerables" who have just given birth, or suffered an amputation. Inevitably, the operation is brutal. A military official threatens to shut down all MSF and Merlin (MSF's British sister organization) operations if they do not cooperate, if the refugees are not moved out immediately.

The following morning, the army begins to confiscate private vehicles to help move the refugees. A few days later, in Kigali, the thoughtful manager of MSF's Rwandan emergency teams, Aaron, admits he was annoyed to find that this diktat included several MSF Land Cruisers. Still, he commented laconically that if it was "irritating," the authorities still appeared to be doing their best to facilitate the evacuation. Far worse, he thinks, is when they close the medical way stations and take sick people off rehydration. "Personally, in the grand scale of things, I think the government has done a pretty good job of returning five hundred thousand refugees." Nevertheless, his concern is now that by hurrying home the refugees – some of whom may be infected with various diseases – "they are risking the spread of cholera."

But the journalists are growing unhappy: they were promised more than a fine photo opportunity. The catastrophic predictions of the two hundred international aid agencies operating in Rwanda left them expecting many deaths, but not enough refugees are sick or dying to satisfy their sanguinary expectations. Feeling cheated, they search for a new story, finding one in questioning the validity of the "crisis," speculating on how much stage-management there has been. "The implosion of the Empire of the Equator is the real story here, not the return of a bunch of refugees," says an intense and gifted Belgian journalist. "After all, the Zairean central government has ceased to exist." He demands reassurance that this so-called "great refugee crisis" is a crisis at all. He was here in Rwanda in 1994, when there really *was* a crisis: first the genocide that left a half-million or more dead, and then what has come to be called "The Judgement" – the cholera that killed thousands more as the refugees streamed into Zaire. But now there is neither genocide nor plague, only the aid agencies' most visible yet damning product – good television footage of the relatively healthy, UN-fed refugees tramping home.

Or they turn their attention to other issues. One journalist says MSF's greatest strength is also its greatest weakness – its ability to get in there *instantly* with on-the-spot and flexible plans can also mean MSF wastes energy by leaping into a country without a thorough assessment of the problem. He notes that hundreds of tons of supplies were brought in by MSF, but demands to be told in what useful way they are being used – and, after all, he has a right to demand such information, for the European Union finances much of this activity. Where *are* these supplies? He does not know that the MSF supplies are in the Kigali warehouses, distributed among MSF stations when appropriate, or shared when needed with other aid agencies. He dismissed the MSF rehydration way stations, ignoring the many who might have died of dehydration without the rehydration salts. "They don't need it – it's rained heavily every day since the move," he insists.

Another journalist has reservations about the new Rwandan government's proclaimed attitude to human rights, but it is difficult to determine if his concern is genuine or merely that of yet another aggrieved Belgian nationalist moaning that his country has once again backed the wrong horse. Nevertheless, he quite legitimately wishes to know if the new Rwandan government will carry out its vow not to impose the notion of "collective guilt" on all Hutus, innocent and guilty alike. Will innocent Hutu women and children be declared guilty, as the Israelis do with the Arabs – because "Oh, they sheltered the killers" or "Oh, they took part in the looting"? Can the new government control the Tutsis' natural desire for revenge? Does it really want to? That week, the international press begins to complain that the suspected killers imprisoned in Kigali are not being swiftly tried. But how could they be since the *genocidaires* murdered most of Rwanda's judges and lawyers and, in the process, dismantled the legal system?

Despite the continuing reaffirmation of the Hutu militants' only apparent political goal – completing the genocide of the Tutsis – and despite the massacres of Hutus by Tutsis and their allies in neighbouring Zaire and the slaughter of many Tutsis inside Rwanda by Hutu terrorists, the new minority Tutsi military government of Rwanda clings precariously to its impossible dream of imposing a non-racist democracy on an alienated Hutu majority.[15]

The Pitiful Remains

Seventeen months after the holocaust of April–June 1994, one week after our visit to the Zairean border, we head south from Kigali along the red-earth road that is stained with the blood of so many murders. Our plan is to spend one full day among the massacre sites. Within five kilometres of the city, the road curves and there on our left is what is now Nyanza cemetery: in this field, hundreds of distraught children, women, and men had huddled together for that illusion of security that comes with being in a crowd. Still, the killers appeared. Those who tried to flee, as well as those who stayed frozen in place, were hacked to death by Interhamwe machetes, hoes, knives. Alleged *genocidaire* Leon Mugasera had told his people to kill all the Tutsis and dump their corpses in the Nyabarongo River

so they can float back to "where they came from," an allusion
to the myth that the Tutsis originally came from Ethiopia. In
the rivers, the slim Tutsi male corpses float face down; the
more generously proportioned Tutsi women's bodies float face
up. Now there are only rows of crosses at what is Nyanza
cemetery, each cross crudely lettered with the name of the
victim and the date of his or her murder – the date is always
the same: April 11, 1994.

BURASANZAYE INNOCENT – 1956 – 11th April 1994

We cross a bridge over the river. There are multilingual
signs and warnings everywhere along the muddy riverbank:
DANGER – MINES! Red flags on sticks serve as extra warning
for those who can neither read nor recognize the symbols. For
some shell-shocked survivors, even that will not be enough,
and they will occasionally stumble onto a minefield.

At mid-morning, we arrive at Nyarama church, the closest
to Kigali of the three massacre sites that Rwandans now col-
lectively call "The Churches." First, the children, women,
and men were machine-gunned on this holy ground, then
rifle grenades burst holes through the walls to give the killers
free access to the hundreds cringing within the church. Most
were assassinated with pangas, which often sliced across the
eyes and through the skull with savage force – easiest to do
with thin-skulled children. The exhausted machete-wielders
frequently took time out for cigarette breaks and a snack as
the dwindling band of blood-soaked survivors inside the

church clawed their way under decapitated and disembowelled bodies to escape the machetes, or tried to bolt to freedom through the door, only to be cut down within metres. They say the massacre took six screeching hours to finish, from eight in the morning until well after lunch.[16]

Eighteen months later, all that remains inside the church are the skeletons, left as a memorial on the spot where they fell. Their flesh has been greedily devoured by the heat and the African armies of insects, worms, and feral dogs. Some women's scarves are still wrapped around their skulls. All else is a jumble of red-dusted bones, pottery gourds, rags, plastic water jugs, cooking pots, cardboard boxes emblazoned with "Coaster Brand Margarine – Product of Holland," and twisted, rusted tins. In some private ceremony, six skulls have been lifted from the floor of the charnel house and placed on what once had been the altar. Behind the macabre altar is the only remaining stained glass in the building, half its blue-veined panes shot out. On the wall are paintings of the Stations of the Cross, but the biblical story seems dwarfed by the Calvary of the Rwandan people.

In one hastily constructed outbuilding, skulls have been carefully piled in rows on broad tables, with that curious Rwandan mixture of reverence and fatalistic indifference. Bones and clothes are stacked on planks the length of the building. Long-dead flowers and wreaths, shrivelled in the scorching Central African sun, recall an earlier attempt to honour the remains. In another shed behind the church are the pitiable inanimate possessions, the remains of what had been hundreds of human beings – clothing, shoes, cups, and sheets all scattered in an unidentifiable jumble, as in an urban refuse dump, or a Nazi concentration camp.

⌐

A Rwandan caretaker asks us to sign the visitors' book and write a comment. Numbed by what we have seen, I can only pretentiously call for "First Justice, and then Reconciliation." Later in the car, I ask our driver, Hassan: "But can there ever be reconciliation?" He is a thoughtful man and, like most Tutsis, thinks carefully before he speaks. "It will be hard, but yes. We could have revenge, but we are not animals. We are men." I am staggered by his apparent generosity of spirit: two of his brothers were murdered nearby, in a previous pogrom.

⌐

Gripped by the waves of intense nausea that now came upon us and would not leave until we returned to Canada, we arrive at the second of "The Churches," Nyamata. This had been built on the outskirts of a sleepy village in the country, and the church itself is a part of a complex of church-built buildings that include a school and a community hall. Here, too, hundreds of Tutsis sheltered. Interhamwe explosives broke through the iron-barred doors that protected them, and the massacre began.

Now, inside the church, its ceiling salted with bullet holes, the Rwandan government prepares a memorial to the genocide. The hundreds of bodies have been kept in fusty, dark plastic bags stacked on one side of the church while they await their communal entombment. Villagers dig inside for what will be the nation's most holy commemoration, for the mass grave will be in the centre of the church. Perhaps thirty metres long, fifteen metres wide, and ten metres deep, it will constitute the underfloor, centrepiece, and holy altar of the reconstructed church. For eternity, the feet of the worshippers will touch the soil that touches the victims' bodies and their blood. Eight men toil in the dust-choked hole, digging with pick and shovel. One stained-glass window and a statue of the Virgin Mary have survived intact. A clipboard-bearing Rwandan official on a bicycle tries to shoo us away, but Hassan intervenes on our behalf. Perhaps simply being here is to take part in a pornography of death, but I wish to freeze this scene in my mind. Outside the church, a wire-service newsman snaps at his wife for being so self-absorbed as to ask for a Kleenex in this holy place.

Early in the afternoon, we head back towards Kigali. We have only travelled a few hundred metres north of the town when the first of the Zairean refugees appear all the way from the north: the Hutus are returning! At first only a few arrive, dispersed as they walk along the road. As we continue north, many more refugees begin to trickle in along the road. Soon truckloads appear, the trucks disgorging their passengers, who head in the direction of their long-abandoned homes.

Some of the refugees are innocent victims of the chaos and dislocation that followed the 1994 genocide; others are the killers. It is impossible to distinguish one from the other – least of all by the blank expressions on their faces, which reveal little of what they have experienced or what they are feeling. They will endure problems when they finally reach their homes: many will find their houses already occupied, and the rights to their property in dispute. The government announces that after each returnee is "registered," he will be permitted to put up a tent in the garden of "his" house for a period of three months, while his claim is processed.

On our way back to Kigali, we stop again at Nyanza cemetery, standing in the rows of crosses – April 11, 1994 – to watch the tide of refugees return. In the centre of the cemetery, surrounded by the field of wooden crosses, is a mass grave covered with cement blocks, now planted with flowers around its borders. The returning refugees file past on the road: some stare vacantly at us while others plod on with determination. Some of them are killers, we must remind ourselves. As they pass, the impenetrable Hassan stands in the cemetery facing the road – his family had fled to exile in Uganda when his brothers were cut to bits. Hassan's arms stretch behind his back, one hand clutching the bicep of the other arm: he looks impassively over their heads, searching for we know not what.

Site of massacre of Tutsis in 1994, Nyarama church, Rwanda.

Hassan: members of his family were killed in the massacre.

Returning Hutus file past cemetery.

2

At the Centre of the World

To be here, at the centre of the world, amongst a half-million survivors of genocide or plague . . . and to act.

Msf is an independent organization, and it sends its personnel anywhere in the world, whenever it learns there is a humanitarian crisis. People often look at MSFers with awe – or with bewilderment ("They must be crazy!"). They see women and men who abandon comfortable sinecures in Canada and Europe to heal the sick in filthy, mud-floored "hospitals" and plastic-sheeted tents – often under the most savage and rat-ridden conditions, tormented by extremes of heat or cold, and bitten by poisonous snakes and insects. They calmly go about their business in the midst of Third World genocides, plagues, famines, and floods; dispatching fellow MSFers to new posts with the

Opposite: MSF doctor, Goma, Zaire.

perplexing traditional adieu: "Have fun!" Most commonly in an emergency they might have dry toast and coffee for breakfast and hurry a meal in the evening, sleeping for a few hours before returning to work the following morning fuelled only by yet another cup of coffee and more dry toast. All this for an airline ticket, free room and board, and the paltry MSF salary of a few hundred dollars each month.

The workers will sometimes be stricken with malaria (three were returned to Canada in one month alone) or diarrhea, and run the risk of contracting from their patients the other exotic diseases they must treat: typhoid, cholera, Kala-Azar. More frightening still, from Chechnya to Yugoslavia, from Rwanda to Cambodia, they increasingly become targets for the local death squads, as political factions begin to see them as useful pawns in the political process and as dangerous witnesses to their activities.

It is only natural that persons who voluntarily embrace such hazards to their own health and well-being, and do so at such personal cost, might be seen as heroes or saints pursuing their own private, perhaps mystical, visions. MSFers themselves sometimes reveal an ambivalence about their image that manifests itself when they tell their war stories to the public. Frank, a Canadian M.D. who often walked alone and unarmed into the Zairean jungle with his medical kit on his back, remembers being held captive for three hours while drunken militiamen fought over the soap he carried in his backpack. After escaping, he remembers that all he could think of was, What am I doing here? I'm catching the next

MSF cholera hospital, Goma, Zaire.

plane home. But as the adrenalin and the shaking fear left his body, so did the desire to abandon his mission. Jean, another Canadian physician, recalled being with other blonde medical workers in a Kurdish refugee camp in Turkey, over-hearing Turkish army soldiers planning to break down their doors and rape them. "We shouted," and made tough and angry noises, she recalled. To put it into a kind of perspective, as if to make light of it, she adds, "Well, they were just going to rape us, not kill us."

Yet nothing irritates MSFers more than being called heroes. They know very well that they are no such thing. In the safety of Nairobi, when Robert learned of the book I was writing, he asked sardonically, with that cutting arrogance of the young, "More heroes, I suppose? It's not as dangerous as it looks from far away, you know. It's our parents who fear the dangers, and imagine them, not us." Most others emphatically insist that heroic – even idealistic – motivation is not in them.

This is no false modesty. In fact, likely candidates for sainthood are as few and far between in MSF as elsewhere, and the motivations for joining are various and often quite mundane – including unemployment or underemployment at home, rebellion against the boredom of a conventional life, or a thirst for adventure and meaning. Few seem to miss their other lives, awash in the ennui of dispensing pills and pre-scriptions, bedpans and bandages for the largely self-inflicted wounds of an industrial nation's secure and overfed popula-tion. Yet there appears to be some private, perhaps secret, certainly rarely articulated, satisfaction that engages and sustains MSFers through their arduous duties. There must be, since in 1994 alone there were 2,950 MSFers working in sixty-four countries, from Afghanistan to Zimbabwe. And MSFers return to their posts again and again, sometimes for years.

⌒

Martin is a physician with MSF (France), one who speaks and writes eloquently of the meaning of his work. Many women find him darkly handsome, but the style of this smouldering and intense physician is wild-eyed – more street person than medical doctor in his clothing, his behaviour, and especially his smell. It is his aroma that precedes him in a room, a reek unfamiliar to anyone who has not lived in the Third World – an odour, a palpable presence of smoky charcoal fires, animal dung, oily mud, and dubious latrines that insinuates itself into the very fibres of unscrubbed clothing, shoe leather, and hair.

Martin is the MSF medical coordinator for all of Zaire, and with ten years' service under his belt he is one of the few true veterans in the business. Indeed, he has been around MSF for so long that everyone knows him. Most respect him from a distance, but a few begrudge him his appeal, while still others speak without fondness of him and his unnecessarily "strong opinions." Sitting at an MSF conference in early November 1996 at the University of Toronto, he seems utterly unaware of how bizarre his behaviour must seem to us as he draws the collar of his jean jacket over his mouth in unconscious imitation of some Transylvanian count, or methodically wraps, unwraps, and then wraps again a scarf around his wrist as if it were a bandage.

Martin feels uncomfortable outside the highly politicized and francophone environment of MSF (France); and he remarks that he remains with the French section because that is where the most intense efforts are consistently made to "analyse, debate and understand what is really going on" in the Third World. Each member nation within MSF is perceived as having its own distinctive flavour: the founding nation, France, with its intellectual roots in the Left, is seen as risk-taking and political, for example, while Holland is technocratic and routinized in its delivery of services. Nevertheless, if Martin feels somehow French, he is in fact a Canadian of Greek ancestry who grew up in Montreal: MSFers are no more bound to serve their own nation's section than a member of the Blue Jays baseball team must be "from" Toronto.

"I am no longer a communist," he says matter-of-factly, as if one is assumed to have been one, but he thinks that in the modern world "there is too much high and low, and not enough dignity." He was working as a labour organizer in Kitimat, British Columbia, when, at the age of twenty-five, he first learned of the existence of MSF. He immediately quit his union job and returned to Quebec, where he enrolled first in a community college and then went on to medical school. Despite this speed, he bemoans the loss of years of potential service while studying medicine: "I should have done nursing instead – it's only three years instead of five – I wasted too much time in university."

"It's not that you decide to do something heroic," he says about his motivation, "it's that you come to realize it's your personal destiny." "Much of our work," he says about his own life's work, "is symbolic and emotional, the contact between the suffering and an expatriate, one human eye contact." He seems obsessed with MSF, and indeed it appears to be the sum total of his identity. "Get our image out," he exhorts his colleagues at the Toronto meeting. "Be visible and recruit more people. That's the important thing for us. We have to go and get it." MSF's historic and ethical responsibility, he tells us, is first to bear witness to these genocides and famines for the world, then to help, and finally to assess more efficient ways of getting aid to the suffering. If MSF may claim to be fundamentally "non-political," humanitarian emergencies are usually caused by politics – so MSF must speak out, regardless of the risk to the organization. The only reason he thinks Europe "survived" the Second World War was the justice dispensed at the Nuremberg trials, followed by the Marshall Plan's vital economic rebuilding of the continent. "Starving people carry grudges," he says. Thus, Martin sums up, the task of MSF is: Bear witness. Give food, water, latrines, medicine.

His one complaint is that MSF is too short on internal dialogue: "I've received three newsletters in five years, and one Christmas card." He eats little at our breakfast, and just before he disappears (leaving behind only his smoky aura), he urges us to help drag Canada into the world, make Canadians

see the suffering of the people of this planet, not help construct more inflated, artificial "MSF heroes."

"A Culture of Its Own"

Many more MSFers, however, would share the pragmatic
views of Leslie, a thirty-three-year-old blonde Canadian M.D.
working in Zaire. "There aren't many naïve idealists in MSF,"
she told journalist Bruce Wallace. "I can't imagine doing a
run-of-the-mill family practice after this. At home, the shooting and shelling sounds horrible, but here you just deal with
it. Look, there are a lot of people who do this because they
can't get a job at home, or at least they can't get an interesting
job at home. Over here, people in their twenties are handed
huge responsibilities: a chance to manage huge budgets, big
staffs. Nobody comes here to help 'the poor and the suffering' any more, and I'm so tired of people asking me, 'How
can you do this?' We like this work. We like the lifestyle. It's
a culture of its own. I find it so difficult with my friends in
Canada when I go back because they don't follow what goes
on in these places. That's why a lot of people in this business
sign on for mission after mission – because they find you just
can't go home." [17]

Sometimes the expressed motives seem very specific.
Gary, a former helicopter pilot who is now a country manager
in Central Africa (our telephone call to him in Burundi was
drowned out by the shriek of incoming artillery fire), writes

Hutu refugees walk cross-country when the roads are blocked.

Somali refugees in MSF *cholera hospital, Dadaab, Kenya.*

Above and opposite: MSF *doctor treating Somali patients, Dagehalla refugee camp, Dadaab.*

MSF cholera hospital, Dadaab.

MSF hospital, Ifo camp, Dadaab.

Somali refugee, Ifo camp, Dadaab.

Hutu refugees near Ruhengeri, Rwanda.

Hutu refugees, Gisenyi, Rwanda.

Hutu cholera patient in isolation, MSF hospital, Gisenyi, Rwanda.

about "the dedication" he encounters everywhere in MSF. "I really believe in what I'm doing now. I spent a lot of years doing international work that I didn't find rewarding. I want to get my hands dirty and [my] feet sloppy." Charles, a member of an emergency team, needs the continuous shock of an adrenalin high: "I tried hang-gliding, then sky-diving, then the State Emergency Services. I want to live on the edge! You're at the border with all those people running towards you, you don't stick to your 'job description.'"

Belgian press officer Annette emphasizes the intoxicating experience: "*Adventure!* You get a lot of responsibility at a very young age." British press officer Amanda thinks many join MSF to escape from boredom: "It's more fun than sitting in an office. After running a hospital and doing surgery, you could never be a nurse in Europe and wear your funny little hat again." Amanda's "worst nightmare is to be married with two children and a mortgage. I love Africa. Here, everything is real, not phony, it's life or death." She gives herself "another year, perhaps two" in MSF, "then you burn out – it's the money, you have no money, and you have no life."

As night falls, we share a meal in Kigali's other reopened restaurant with a flamboyant South American photo-journalist who joyously complains that "every time I come to Rwanda, I get shot," referring thus to his tendency to jump into the heart of a firefight if it will yield a great photograph. Amanda affirms the same hypnotic attraction: "I love MSF. You meet so many interesting people. You're in a little country that nobody gives a damn about and you learn so much about it, and know everybody. I love it. I'd like to live in all these different countries. I'd go crazy if I was in one place."

Others express their commitment to the physical discomfort, the risk, and the punitive salary with tales that mix sentiment with a taste for the exotic. The shambling German giant, Völker, toils as a logistician for MSF in the bandit-ridden, snake- and scorpion-infested Sudan, in temperatures that can approach fifty degrees. Like most MSFers, he smokes constantly, rolling by hand his sweet-scented Dutch shag tobacco, smoking even in bed. Occasionally he sets his mosquito net on fire, shouts his characteristic "damn shit!" and stuffs a sock or two into the hole. Habitually shod in his enormous, unlaced hunting boots, he struggles to explain: "When I first came, a boy and all his friends they walked by my side and held my hand everywhere – that's what kept me going in the business." He even reaches for a touch of glamour, as when the MSF radio informed Völker that "Judith Charlie" was arriving in his wilderness Sudanese camp, he wondered, Who the hell is Judith Charlie? "You'll know when you see him," the operator replied, and when the light plane landed in the barren desert, former American president Jimmy Carter emerged, surrounded by his Secret Service men in their obligatory three-piece suits and sunglasses.

Still others express a political motivation. Cathy, a Canadian press officer, hopped from one segment of "the movement" (the term she uses to refer to all progressive social activists, from feminists to collectivists to ecologists) to another. She joined MSF after a stint with Antarctic eco-tourism, and another on a collective farm in then-Soviet Armenia. When I asked why she cared so much, she was overcome with emotion and shouted, "Don't! You'll make me cry," before bolting to another room to sob. "That was a good question," she said when she returned, having collected herself. "That was a good answer," replied Greg Locke. Maria, an intense and introverted Spanish M.D. clad in her poncho, squirms with embarrassment at the mere prospect of being interviewed while I gently urge her to recall: "I finished my medical degree in '86. I was a researcher. I was offered a position in Nicaragua in '91, and since then I'm hooked with this job. [I do it] because I strongly believe in human beings still, and in cooperation. I learned that in Managua in '91."

Others remain despairingly mute. In the slums of Nairobi, Sidney, an agronomist, explains why she no longer tries to explain: "You cannot transmit why you care to most people." Her colleague Cynthia, a nurse, encourages me through discouragement: "I think you have taken a most difficult job – to try to make people understand." I do not tell her that it is *me* I am trying to enlighten, not others.

Some are explicitly spiritual in motivation. In a sophisticated, modern hospital near the Burundi border, Georg, an ethereal and charismatic Scandinavian physician built like a soccer player, talks about the unanticipated consequences of aid agencies' efforts in the Third World. "In fact, our work here has less practical effect than in Norway. I don't see this work as being more useful, or productive – it's not that." What matters most to him flows from his profound and contagious spirituality. "I can take part in a transcultural reaching out of a hand – putting yourself at their disposal as a sign of respect, that's what it's basically about. We don't really know what our impact is, but it's an attitude we want to propagate. We want to break barriers across borders. We are very good at what we're doing, and we are motivated in a way that government agencies will never be because they're paid for it. It's not a commitment to them. That's our real strength."

His colleague, Belgian M.D. Carmen, claims to come for more pragmatic reasons: doctors are often underemployed in Belgium, but "you have a lot to do when you are a surgeon in Africa." She takes great pride in the grisly tasks she must perform in this war, the special expertise she has developed for dealing with the victims of torture and mutilation. She also seems almost to relish the privations she endures. "It's difficult. You forget to take your pills, so I have malaria. And I have open wounds on me." During the genocide in 1994, her biggest job "was to suture the tendons where they had cut off the hands." Now, in the killing zone that is the Rwanda–Burundi border, in an atmosphere of frequent attacks on civilians and military alike, with the bullet-riddled and the freshly amputated moaning in her surgery, she rejoices in the opportunity to give aid and succour. "The people came to us, the only thing you can do is improve the people in an emergency."

"I wanted to come," says tiny French nurse Nancy, sheltering from the heavy rain in a windswept tent in the north of Rwanda, with rivulets of soupy mud swirling onto the floor.

At home, she nurses in Bourdeaux, and at first she "had mixed feelings" about joining MSF. "I wanted to help, but I didn't know what could be done. I'm a nurse, I can have a job in France, not like the logisticians." She talks to us as she continues to work, feeling foreheads and bandaging wounds. She joined MSF rather than other aid agencies "because of its professionalism, its speed, they know how to do their jobs and what equipment they need. Your energy has much more results here than in France – multiplied many times. I like my job in France, but it is difficult to top this."

MSF

MSF was founded in France in 1971, when the radicalism of the 1960s had temporarily transformed the consciousness of an entire generation in the western world. A group of disillusioned French doctors and journalists returned to Paris from a Red Cross mission to the Biafran War and created Médecins Sans Frontières/Doctors Without Borders. MSF would quickly become the world's largest private, independent emergency medical relief organization, charged with speaking out against human-rights violations and providing medical assistance wherever it is needed. The Canadian branch was founded in 1991, and since then several hundred Canadians have worked in dozens of countries around the world. Worldwide, MSF has six major sections: Holland, France, Belgium, Switzerland, Spain, and Luxembourg. Thirteen nations including Canada have affiliate status – Canada being funded and administered primarily from Holland.

The name of Médecins Sans Frontières (and the anglicized Doctors Without Borders) is an unfortunate linguistic capitulation to the prestige of physicians in the modern world. Perhaps for reasons of public relations, it explicitly states that this is an organization of M.D.s. In fact, MSF is much more than that: it is nurses, not doctors, who do much of the actual hands-on medical work; it is water and sanitation specialists, nutritionists, and epidemiologists who make the largest contribution to public health; and it is logisticians and administrators, plumbers and radio operators, lawyers, mechanics, and accountants who ensure that the essential medicines, food, petrol, personnel, vehicles, water bladders, and tools are delivered to those in the heart of the emergency. Inside the organization, this equality of contribution is implicitly recognized in the universal absence of titles and the routine use of first names – practices that discourage that social distancing, that lack of intimacy and work-team harmony, the disincentive to cooperate inherent in the use of reminders of the outside world's status hierarchy.

Inside MSF, the informal prestige hierarchy is based less on what its members do – less on the fine distinctions of rank the world makes between doctors and nurses, logisticians and administrators – than on where they have served. Arriving at a new station or in a new country, they introduce themselves the way abused Yanomamo wives sometimes compare scalp scars – with a perverse pride in the catalogue of what they have endured, and where. "I worked in the Ivory Coast for twelve months, in Afghanistan, then in the bloody mess in Bosnia," says one as she walks for the first time through the upcountry Rwandan MSF station door and proffers her credentials. The longer the list and the more dangerous the locations, the more prestige will implicitly be hers. Distinctions are also made according to the length of time served. The ten-year veteran, Martin, admits he sometimes feels profoundly different from short-termers who sign up for a month in an emergency but maintain their comfortable lives at home.

In unstressed times, MSF recruits its people through conventional means, cautiously matching persons to niches – thus a mechanical engineer in civilian life becomes a water and sanitation specialist, or perhaps an administrator. But in times of crisis, people can be hurriedly recruited, as with one MSF legend, a tattooed giant with purple hair who had run a biker bar in Montreal. Virtually plucked from a street in Paris, he found himself on a plane to Malawi to organize the construction of a cholera camp, a task he accomplished with celebrated discipline and *élan*.

In the frenzy of an emergency, calculated risks are taken by both MSF and the recruits. Sylvia, a redheaded British nutritionist, accepted a short-term appointment as administrator of a tiny, out-of-the-way border post in Rwanda, scant days before all political calculations changed and a half-million refugees surged down the road towards her. Suddenly, dozens of medical workers were Sylvia's responsibility, camping in her rooms, demanding her food and supplies.

Swedish doctor and MSF staff at a cholera camp.

MSF logistician and driver.

Similarly, the young Belgian nurse, Barbara, found herself in the Rwandan crisis forced to serve as a radio operator – buoyed up only by her commitment and her playful sense of humour, as when she teasingly urged us to calm the five-inch, lobster-clawed, flying biting beetles infesting the house by "caressing their necks." Finally, when a qualified radio technician was found weeks later, Barbara was ecstatic to learn that she would be released into an especially dangerous temporary hospital in Zaire. Exceptions, too, are made for veterans: Ronald, a long-serving and widely loved country transport manager who messes about in West Indian yachts for several months each year, ran out of sailing berths and was instantly dispatched by MSF to a second tour of duty in Rwanda when he signalled for help.

MSF especially needs doctors' skills for an assessment of the overall medical situation and for the organization of the emergency health-care services that will often actually be delivered by nurses and their local assistants. It is *nurses* who do much of the actual tending to patients – the preliminary diagnoses and the emergency treatment of all trauma and disease. An academic epidemiologist from a European medical school will monitor an endangered population for signs of any outbreaks of contagious diseases, and make recommendations to MSF based upon his scientific observations. But, at the same time, a man who once worked in a bank in Europe learns to become a food-security specialist whose job is a careful "anthropological" assessment – based on a knowledge of the culture's mechanisms for the production and circulation of food – of the nutritional needs of a population radically disturbed by massacre, starvation, plague, and flight.

A water and sanitation specialist may have no formal training of any direct relevance, but his contribution to public health is arguably the most essential "medical" task of all: clean water free from plague, initially flown in from Europe or Canada in giant multi-thousand-litre bladders the size of a living room; and the digging of a simple public latrine to restrict the spread of disease. He may have a B.A. in geography or anthropology, but he will develop his skills on demand. A press officer may be a committed social activist who has written a book on the plight of women in Tibet; or she may be the kind of elegant and media-aware spokesperson that some European commentators have dismissed as "catastrophe babes," handing out their cards and their organization's propaganda at every world crisis. A logistician, without whom none of the MSF services can be provided, may once have been a mechanic or a businessman, but now utilizes that special organizational mental timbre that can simultaneously juggle the conflicting needs of hundreds of specialists in "his" country.

Country managers and heads of missions oversee all MSF operations in a country, including negotiating with the current government for free access, and with rebel factions for guarantees of safety. They are as likely to have been a nurse or a doctor as a mechanical engineer, a helicopter pilot or a B.A. (Honours) in classical studies. Thus, the manic Patrick served first as a nurse with the U.S. army in Vietnam before becoming a Trappist monk, then a graduate student in philosophy, and ultimately a senior MSF administrator. MSF lawyers negotiate with national governments and world bodies and support the "humanitarian claims to access to populations in danger, advise on the human right to medical treatment and personal security," says Alphonse, as well as offering more mundane services to governments regarding the "maintenance of the charity tax status, protection of trademarks and logos, legal aspects of fund-raising, and staff recruitment."

"Just Strange Things, Crazy Things, Please!"

Whatever function MSFers provide will reflect both their temperaments and abilities as well as MSF's immediate needs as it responds to crises around the world. Charles, a frenetic thirty-three-year-old Australian emergency field coordinator with formal training in automotive mechanics, perches on a steamer trunk in MSF's Kigali headquarters and tries to summarize the dizzying blur that is his career. "When I finished college, I left home and lived in the street in Sydney. I was a bit worried the gangs were going to kill me, so I went to the States and got a job with the blind and handicapped. I was a Seventh-day Adventist then. I'm a water diviner, too. Then I helped build a bridge across the Mekong River to Laos. I *love* water and water development. I tried an M.Sc. degree, but eight weeks later I was so restless I quit and went to New

Guinea to teach in primary school, then got a job with World Vision in Sudan, then to Europe, then the United Nations Humanitarian Rights Commission in Bangladesh. I finished that contract, but I was very disappointed because the UN was so bureaucratic it took three months to make any decisions. So I went with MSF (Holland) in 1992 to Somalia, then I came back to Holland, then Khartoum, where there were floods, then the war crisis in Liberia, then Angola, then to Pakistan and Bangladesh for floods. I came here during the war, trying to set up a field hospital while we were being shelled at the airport – I still recognize those holes. Then I went to Goma in Zaire to organize the water trucks, a record – two million litres a day – then Bosnia, and into Liberia to set up MSF. Then I applied to Oxford University for an M.A. in development practices, emergency – a new program. I had a holiday in Australia for a month, via Indonesia, where my fiancée was killed – politics – and then to Thailand, where there is a girl whose parents made sure she married a Thai – I have a lot of difficulty in opening up to that. At the moment, there is a girl in Amsterdam who says she has loved me for two years, so she is coming with me to Australia." As I leave his company, he hands me his lengthy résumé, which shows how many jobs in how many continents he has not even bothered to mention.

Their occupational histories are rarely as bizarre as Charles', but they are infinitely varied. Self-mocking MSF accountant Ronald was in business in Europe, running a chain of Rent A Cars and "making a fortune." When his father told him "you should do something more important," he tried impressing him by joining MSF. Now his father mindlessly repeats his complaint. Ronald daydreams of buying his own sailboat and going back to the West Indies, anchoring it a few hundred metres from shore and for all eternity hitting golf balls off a mat towards the beach. Yet most of his life is in fact confined to a tiny room in the heart of MSF headquarters in Kigali, connected to the world only by fax, computer, and telephones. "I never leave this office," he jokes. "For all I know, all my colleagues are not doing *any* of the things they say they are and that I give them the money for. How would I know if they were really doing it, anyway? I never leave this office." It is eight o'clock in the morning, and he punches and repunches the telephone, trying with mounting frustration to reach people: "Why can you never get people at this time of day?"

Jean, a physician who has just married a wealthy Canadian businessman, is out of active service for the immediate future, and she now serves on the MSF post-operations psychological support network. Georg, a Swedish M.D., has a medical practice in Norway with two colleagues who cover for him during his periodic stints with MSF. Jacque-Paul, a food-security specialist for ten years, admits to being "the fossil" of MSF (Belgium). He worked for a period as a travel guide, then "I was working in a bank, in 1986, I wanted to travel, and I went to MSF and the other NGOs [non-governmental organizations], but they were much slower and MSF was the first one that called me. They gave me one week [to prepare] – I was in

Ethiopia, Sudan, Angola, Mozambique, and Rwanda in support missions, first as a logistician." His wife, an M.D., is also with MSF. "We meet often enough to make a baby, but for the long term we try to get the same posting."

Solid and unflappable MSF logistician Goose was trained as a mechanical engineer: after a stint in the Dutch army, he joined a multinational corporation. "I worked one year for Shell Oil. If you work for Shell, you know what you're going to do for the rest of your life. 'What's your five-year plan?' they ask you. They actually ask each other questions like that! I don't want anything, write that down! And I said to myself, 'No more real work, no long-term plans or commitments. Just strange things, crazy things, please!' So I looked in a newspaper. I decided to be a travel guide in France, but I met a guy who worked with MSF. My first question to him was 'Are you a doctor?' and he said, 'No,' and I said, 'Well, we have something in common, I'm not a doctor, either.' He said he's a logistician – organizing houses, cars, and electricity – and that rang a bell with me because that was like what I was doing in the army. We in MSF are an army, we try to be independent, even to generate our own electricity. So I thought, Okay, that fits, it fits exactly. I just knew it. I was looking for something like this.

"First, I started as interim head of mission in Nairobi, then to Kampala to look at our accessibility into Zaire, then we were flooded with refugees and found we had to set up way stations, then they asked me to be the country manager for truck transport, then quick back to Kampala to link up with a medical mission to Zaire, then when we got no government permission from Zaire, it was back to Kampala, where I served as liaison officer. And I came back here to Kigali and I'm logistician for the flights coming into here." Indeed, Goose "drilled wells in Thailand, built schools in Guatemala, and lectured at the University of Fiji on mechanical engineering. Then I was with the logging industry in the Solomon Islands, and in Afghanistan as the negotiator with the rebels. A logistician organizes everything, [even] which room they sleep in, so people need you, and most of the time you pull all the wires. To be a good logistician you should be a jack of all trades. You have adrenalin that keeps you going, you sleep only four hours a night, but it keeps you going, you want to do something with your energy. I am not adventurous at all, no way, I want easy, smooth going. Excitement is not in travelling. For relaxing at home in Holland, I drive trucks."

Aaron, the Dutch head of Rwanda's MSF emergency team, came from academe: "I was studying cultural anthropology, I studied my languages, I worked in between. I wasn't really satisfied with the life. Sitting at a bar with a friend who had been in MSF when Somalia was blowing up, I thought, I've found it! MSF bypasses usual [recruitment] procedures in crises, and I said, 'Okay, I'll do it.' Three days later I was in the field in Nairobi." Similarly, Spanish physician Maria was excited at the prospect of working in primitive conditions in the Third World: "It is a very different approach to medicine, there are very different procedures. Most doctors are used to

European hospitals – 'Where is the microscope?' They study academic medicine, not emergency medicine."

Thirty-one-year-old Clive, a Dutch water and sanitation man whose energy seems to radiate through his olive complexion, began his career studying physical geography at Utrecht University, but he found regular jobs too predictable and conventional life too dull. He volunteered seven years ago with MSF and later became a permanent staff member, working in Peru, Zaire, and now in Rwanda. "Eventually, you burn out," he said when I noted how young everyone in MSF seemed to be. He was drafted into the Dutch army in the late 1980s: caught in the throes of adolescent rebellion, he refused to wear a uniform and served instead in the army's "union." Clive said he had no self-confidence when he was younger, but working for MSF let him see what he could and could not do, and in the process define his identity – and through that, gain real self-confidence.

Most took an indirect route. Ivan qualified in medicine at the age of fifty-one after a full career in the Danish army. Now sixty-eight, he has served nine months in Zimbabwe and Mozambique and is back for more in Rwanda, where he will captain the experimental mobile emergency response teams that work out of travelling vans. He insists only that he be home in Denmark for Christmas because his wife cannot shovel the snow, and in any case his ninety-one-year-old father is joining them for the holiday. Ivan said he decided to try medicine when at forty-five he found himself the unlikely second in command of the Danish Atomic/Biological/Chemical Warfare base, and realized that he would be forced onto a pension and a dull life at sixty. "So here I am." Agronomist Sidney works as an MSF community development officer in the Nairobi slums: she had previously worked with women's groups, with tree planting, and with water programs. Soft-spoken and reticent, Ian is an Irish mechanical engineering graduate. After college he took a specialized course in water engineering and has been with various aid agencies ever since, first with the Irish GOAL and now for three years with MSF – first as a logistician to gain experience, now as head of mission in Somalia.

But the demands of working for MSF – inevitably splintered romantic relationships, limited money, uncertain career prospects, and tough and often dangerous conditions – take their toll. With few exceptions, MSFers are overwhelmingly *young*, and their careers are measured in months or years, rarely decades. Two medical workers in Kenya speculated that most MSFers can only handle at most from five to eight years of relief work before moving to a job at head office or returning to regular life. At home in Germany, logistician Völker works as a "consultant logistician" for corporations with warehousing problems: "It's too damn-shit expensive to work for MSF, I'll have to go back to Germany to make some money." What brings them back again and again until they can bear it no more? What reservoir of strength and determination do they draw upon?

The Obliteration of Alienation

A primary quality of life in the modern urban, industrial world is alienation. People are brought to work in the cities, packed together in anonymous apartments, often disconnected from family, from neighbourhood, and, more importantly, from themselves. This process of progressive alienation has its roots in modernity, in the industrialization of the economy, the urbanization of the landscape, and the stratification of society that began in the late eighteenth century and reached its fullest flowering in our time.

The Industrial Revolution was one of the great human achievements. On the one hand, it liberated people, freeing them from otherwise unbreakable social commitments to kin and neighbours, as well as from the unthinkable slaveries of caste, race, gender, and class. Anthropologist Eric Wolf wrote that in liberating people, it made them independent actors, directors of their own lives. Yet it also created its own reservoir of anguish. In the industrializing nineteenth century, both conservative and radical social critics were appalled at the new alienation they saw. In the transformed industrial order, people were alienated from "the product of their work which disappeared into the market"; alienated from "their fellow men who had become actual or potential competitors in the market"; and from "themselves to the extent to which they now had to look upon their own capabilities as marketable commodities," no longer the qualities of a full human being.[18]

This alienation of modern industrial man can cut the spirit like a machete. John Berger, writing of an extreme form of this dilemma in *A Seventh Man* – migrant labouring in wealthy Europe – speaks of it as a form of "imprisonment," wherein a man imported for his labour from the Third World is hermetically sealed off from all natural social and sexual intercourse – with his lover, his family, and his home – and is thus transformed into a kind of non-person. Many MSFers also felt like non-persons when trapped in their dull previous lives.[19]

Becoming an MSFer is the opposite of this experience: it is a kind of *dis*alienation. Membership liberates them as human beings, allows them to explore fully their potential as they seize the opportunity to act. With that liberation comes a profound conviction of the purity of what they do, of the moral superiority of their agency and themselves – a belief so powerful, a satisfaction so intense, that it sustains them through whatever they must do. To witness atrocity and fear, to treat vile diseases, to heal terrible wounds, to dig the latrine or deliver clean water are all part of a process in which they confront reality and construct their identities. In acting thus with such purpose and moral clarity, all other dilemmas dissolve. To act without ambivalence or regret, to cut through the mindlessness of conventional life, to revel in what one is and what one does is for them the only way to become whole.

MSFers do not of course usually discuss their lives in terms of social philosophy. Yet they consistently allude to the trivialization, even negation, of self that comes with being a replaceable "cog in a machine" in Europe or America. Clive

speaks for them all when he reminds us of his gift from MSF
– to be permitted to do something of value, to act with confidence, to create his identity, to seize control of his life.
Through MSF, he can achieve a kind of internal peace through
meaningful labour. He heals himself as he gives the suffering
the means to heal, as he sees firsthand the results of setting up
a water station, supervising the digging of a latrine. When he
works in his characteristic state of total concentration, he is
always smiling.

Now they are with MSF, the elite shock troops of the
unarmed armies of international aid, the firefighters who are
parachuted into a crisis at the first sign of trouble, women and
men who routinely go where modern armies and their political masters fear to tread. Now there is no endless waiting as
a bureaucracy creeps towards an always meaningless and
already outdated decision: MSF makes decisions according to
circumstance, and MSF makes them *now*. If they are at home
on leave, a packed suitcase sits ready by the door, because the
recall could come at any time.

Their work will drain every ounce of their energy. They
will eat and sleep when and where they can, but their being is
engorged with a sense of purpose that transcends their experience, electrifying their muddy and repellent insect- and
reptile-infested environment. We see it all at once on our very
first full day in Africa, as we sit in an outbuilding behind MSF's
East African Logistics Centre in Nairobi. It is now what the
Irish call the edge of dark, and a lone fluorescent bulb on a
wall partly illuminates the shadowy room. All we can hear

in the background is the song of unfamiliar birds and the sudden onset of this minor rainy season's windswept showers. Leaning over Harry's shoulder we surmise that Zaire, the rotten Empire of the Equator, is indeed imploding and a million refugees are about to pour across the border. What rivets our attention is the clicking of Harry's computer keys, and his rapid switches from Dutch to English on the radio-telephone as MSF struggles to estimate the scale of the disaster. In the main building in front of us, Robert is making a flurry of telephone calls around the world to orchestrate emergency flights into Rwanda. Two rooms away, other MSF workers are on radio-telephones, straining for up-to-the-moment information from their workers in the jungle – "Allo? Allo? Allo?" Lizards wait patiently on the wall and gorge on the insects that swarm the light. Thousands of white-winged moths swirl and dance in front of the outdoor lamps. "Stand by . . . over," sputters through the radio. Nothing else for them will ever be so complete, so focused, so absorbing.

When they arrive at their new posting – into the throat of a flood in Somalia, an epidemic in Cambodia, a plague in the Sudan, or a bloody civil war in what once was Yugoslavia – they become part of a self-confident elite. They lose all sense of alienation, they fuse with both their inner beings and their fellows, and become what they wish to be. We're the best; we don't panic; we know what's going on, and we know what we're doing; we're politically and financially independent; and we tell the others just what we think of them. But most of all we work.

We are back in Rwanda with a million refugees pounding down the road from Zaire. As we leave to check the MSF installations, the inexperienced young woman from a UN relief camp radios in a panic: "The refugees are all here, we don't know if we can handle it!" "Ridiculous!" exclaims MSF nurse Monique. "Don't panic! Everything is fine, at least until tomorrow morning. We're not panicking." Later, as the moving wave of refugees appears below our way station, she phlegmatically announces over the radio-telephone, "Okay, they are coming. We are ready for them."

Contact! Not the mindless handing out of food and medicines, but witnessing against evil. Not the soul-less merchandising of public health, but eye and hand contact with the victims of unthinkable deprivation. Their job is clear: Feel the suffering with your hands. Witness, food, water, latrines, medicine!

Contact with the humanity of others and the self's full potential, contact with those who need and feel your human help – the crippled, raped, torn, and traumatized, the victims of ruthless political manipulators. The space around you has become the centre of the world, regardless of whether the eyes of the world are turned in horror on the suffering people before you, as in Rwanda and Zaire in November 1996, or when no one else is watching, as in the unknown wars and genocides in Asia, South America, and Africa. These are the disremembered and unacknowledged tortures, plagues, and famines that only you and your most intimate friends can reach out and touch, and heal. This is the meaning of humanity.

They all share in the intoxication of focused collective action. Make decisions, act to soothe suffering, save lives, to hell with everybody else. A thirsty crowd gathers to watch Clive finish connecting the giant water bladder to its pipes: an audible moan escapes their lips when a tap is turned and a faucet gushes. A few weeks ago, I had thought MSFers were exercising some kind of false modesty when they balked at being called heroes, but now I understand that they are merely experiencing what it is to be fully alive. This is dis-alienation, the antithesis of the programmed numbness that life in a modern industrial city can be, commuting alone to anonymous work with strangers.

Weeks later, Interhamwe death squads will come with murderous intent to the gate of our emergency team's house in Ruhengeri, but will find the doors too awkward to break, the unarmed MSF guards too stubborn. They will go instead a few metres down the road, drag three Spanish medical workers and an American to the lawn, check their passports to ensure they are the inconvenient foreign witnesses to their genocidal evil, and shoot them on the spot. Only the American will escape death, but his leg will be amputated to save his life. As the death squad flees, it will kill three Rwandan soldiers and many civilians.

This night, around a hurried meal in the MSF compound, an intolerable screeching bursts from the hallway, where rats are fighting for food. Monique runs through the kitchen, past the enormous insects in the air and on the table, and confronts the rats as she would the killers. "Fuck off!" she shouts.

Other aid agencies will withdraw from the country immediately after the murders, but MSF workers vote to stay in place for the time being, unarmed, only reminding themselves they are free to leave at any time if they feel insecure.

⌒

It is one month later, and long after dark in Nairobi. We have been driven to the MSF team's home in Priscilla's decrepit Peugeot 405 wagon. Ian enthusiastically says please when Bonnie asks if he wants a coffee, but the cup I leave beside him grows cold as he hunches over his glowing computer in the darkened radio room, analysing Somalian morbidity data. He has forgotten the coffee is there.

MSF worker and Hutu refugees at Goma on the Zaire–Rwanda border.

Album: The Refugees Return

Hutu refugees return to Rwanda from Zaire, November 1996.

When the roads become congested, Hutu refugees take to the fields.

Hutu refugees camp beside the road, Ruhengeri, Rwanda.

3

Emergency Medicine

in the Third World

She is amputating the boy's arm and leg: in a spray of blood and bone chips, the MSF surgeon's saw slices through the devastated tissue. The boy is fourteen. They have removed his right forearm below the elbow, and his right leg below the knee, because a few hours earlier he had with foolish curiosity touched a land mine. Somehow he has managed to cling to life despite the shock and blood loss. Now his severed stumps flop like dead fish over the side of the stretcher as he is carried unconscious out of the operating room. His eyes are closed as we pass him in the corridor of Butare hospital, Rwanda's bombed-to-rubble (and quickly rebuilt) second city on the Burundi border.

Opposite: Hutu father and child at Little Wall Camp, Rwanda.

MSF doctors are highly skilled in such amputations – after all, they do so many of them around the world. Rwandan MSFers are especially experienced in the repair of terrible mutilations, since a favourite Interhamwe tactic is to cut off the victim's hands before (or sometimes in lieu of) the actual killing. Some of the tortured escape in the mêlée with gushing stumps, often permitted to do so for the amusement of their butchers. Carmen is proud of her surgical skill, her ability to save so many limbs and lives, as she should be. She joins us at lunch, but does not share our food. "I do not eat," she says, and a glance at her delicate birdlike frame suggests she may not exaggerate much.

In a hospital ward on our left, a half-conscious woman weakly tries to sit up in bed: her bullet-punctured body slumps forward, her eyes are glazed and unresponsive. Bullets from such high-velocity rounds as the ubiquitous AK-47 devastate living flesh as they ricochet through bone, tissue, and organs. She shivers uncontrollably as her body fights to survive the trauma of such jagged wounds. She and the others in her group – three men, two women, and two children – were attacked as they walked near the border with Burundi. Most have endured multiple hits. They have been shot because of what passes here for a good political reason: random attacks on civilians are the easiest way to "make terror." In Central African wars, the casualties are virtually *all civilians*, since they are safe to wound and kill and, as hostages, can be useful as a shield behind which the armies hide.[20]

It should come as no surprise perhaps that the majority of MSF's doctors and nurses are women. More likely to be deprived of true autonomy and power in their own gender-biased societies, and imbued with that greater humanitarianism of women's culture that dwarfs the cheap careerism of male-dominated institutions, women seem readier to explore their professional lives in an unconventional context. Social commentator Barbara Ehrenreich writes that if modern medicine has eclipsed the role of traditional women healers, women nevertheless continue to be healers. Indeed, modern "scientific" medicine "has lost much of the traditional healer's sense of spiritual commitment and community responsibility.

"In traditional cultures, women are often the principal healers – the first resort against illness or disease. The Latin American *curanderas*, the 'wise women' of the old French countryside, and the midwives who delivered many American babies until well into the twentieth century all represent the ancient tradition of female lay healing. Even in modern societies, mothers are expected to be alert for signs of illness, to nurse the sick, and to monitor the health needs of their families." [21]

It is surely then MSF's medical staff – women and men – who "may help revive the soul of modern medicine." Preternaturally sensitive, almost eerily telepathic (twice she read my expression and laughingly told me what I was thinking – "Oh, I see you are thinking, Look at all these amazing MSFers!"), Dutch nurse Selina, who looks like American actress Shelley Duvall, is training to be a country manager.

Her version of necessary emergency medicine includes far more than coping with medical catastrophe. "Sometimes I think, What are we doing here? Are we doing any good when thirty-eight out of forty of the children we see will be dead, anyway? All this money we spend! But you have to take meaning in the small things, a little help and attention. I had such a special experience: There was a grandmother and her grandchild died in Sudan, and she was alone and she didn't have anybody to help bury the child. I took the people from the Feeding Centre with shovels and I carried the dead child through the rain for one kilometre. It was such an amazing situation. We were sitting down. The child is laying there dead and the grandmother's slipper was broken and while we fixed that she took the big knife and she is cutting her *toenails!* And then we went on. Death is such a part of life here, it's a different ceremony. They dig a hole and lay the child down and fill it up with leaves, and the grandfather said thanks to those that helped them, and they went home."

When Khartoum's years-long drought finally broke, Selina recalls, "it rained eight days and the refugee camp was flooded. The doctor and I gave out medicines to the people, and one woman asked for the empty cardboard box the medicines came in. 'It's empty,' she said. 'It will make a good wall for my house.'" Thus, humanitarian medicine can be "different things," more than medical heroics. "I like to do something for people. In these situations if you are not going to do it, no one will do it – while if I don't go to work in

Holland, another nurse will. And learning how I can survive in different situations. And I like it here as well. Where can you work, to have so many different experiences, to learn so much about yourself as well? What's happening? Can I cope with it? The tension! It's not that we are doing more important things than raising a family or keeping a shop, it's all important. Sometimes I think it would be nice to have a family like my sisters have, but sometimes they think, It would be nice to go everywhere like Selina. You do a lot for yourself, but it's a need for me to do something for other people – but I'm doing it for myself, too."

⌐

From the MSF *Clinical Guidelines Manual*:

Plague: responsible for panedemics in Europe which caused high mortality, large animal reservoirs persist. Extreme care when handling exudates and cadavers.
Malaria: syndromes often found in the same patient [include] convulsions, coma, shock, jaundice, renal failure.
Cholera: an acute, infectious, often fatal disease, characterized by profuse diarrhea, vomiting, cramps.
Kala-Azar: a chronic, usually fatal "wasting" disease characterized by irregular fever, enlargement of the spleen, and emaciation.

Dehydration: the principal reason for the mortality attributable to diarrhea. *Signs:* anxious, clammy, muscle cramps, dizzy if standing.[22]

If ancient epidemics are part of MSF's medical work, so are more mundane (if life-threatening) assaults on the body. In our endless criss-crossing of Rwanda, we find the Scottish nurse, Julie, in a mobile hospital in the north of Rwanda, a simple van trundling along the road searching for the weakest – "the vulnerables" – among the thousands of refugees. Like so many of her colleagues, she is reluctant to be interviewed, even by the gentlemanly British journalist who approaches her – so severe is her discomfort that her face contorts and retreats into a wooden self-consciousness until she is freed to treat the next sick person. Despite her disquiet at our presence, we doggedly follow her to her next stop, a hundred metres square of stinking, rain-soaked mud, shrouded in fog. The smoke from cooking fires and the black diesel fumes from the ancient and ill-maintained vehicles consume what little is left of the air. She grits her teeth and continues with the interview, but the instant she takes her leave from the journalist, the joy on her face returns and her facial paralysis disappears. It is cold today by African standards: people are shivering, but Julie wears only an MSF T-shirt, jeans, and sneakers. She needs nothing more since her feet hardly touch the inch-deep mud as she glides from patient to patient. Anyone who cares to look can see her youthful exuberance, even exultation, to be doing what she knows how to do. So long as she is not forced to talk about it.

It is the minor rainy season in Central Africa, so the daily showers that break the back of the rising heat can be long and furious. Still following Julie's van, we leave the main road – paved years before with international funds and imported Chinese labour – and slither for miles behind her over a soupy hillside track littered with stuck vehicles, one of which appears to have hit a land mine. At Nemba permanent local hospital, a bridge crosses the muddy, chocolate-milky river that completely surrounds the hospital. We cross the little bridge, and stop here because she needs to pick up fresh medical supplies, especially rehydration salts. Her face and body turn once again to stone as she mechanically tells the journalist: "We ended up seeing about fifty people this morning, and we did about twenty dressings. It'd be nice to have a clinic to do things in, but the work we're doing just now changes from morning to evening. We were going to work in Mukungwa camp today, but the authorities moved everybody along, so we had to change our plans and become mobile in the van. We thought we'd see only a few patients, but we've seen diarrhea, malaria, exhaustion, all of it: they've been walking days and days. You have to make the decisions quickly, too – treat the very serious things, first the life threatening diseases."

The slimy mud road to Byumba cuts for miles through the exquisite greens of the terraced and conical Rwandan hills, perpetually topped with black storm clouds in the rainy season. Suddenly, the MSF hospital-van pulls onto a side road on the edge of a village, the rear and side doors spring open, a table is slid out the back, and staff are dispatched to their rehearsed positions. In the bizarre metamorphosis the situation demands, the van is thus transformed into a hospital. Weakened refugees accustomed to the ministrations of the various international aid agencies immediately grasp what is being offered to them. The lame and the halt form a queue behind the van to become part of a medical production line. The first MSF assistant checks for fever by touching each face and chest: where it is indicated, the aide on his right hands out oral rehydrants. Others await bandaging or a medical interview by the side of the van. Indifferent to the ankle-deep mud and the omnipresent rain shower, Julie and her assistant prepare gauze bandages and antiseptic, make dressings for injuries, watch for symptoms of cholera and malaria. They are utterly focused on their work: we have ceased to exist, and there is only a silence, a calm fusion between medical worker and patient.

Near us walks an endless line of refugees, now close to their home communes and villages (or already there). Government soldiers examine each face, watching for the known killers, intensely alert to provocation. An elderly woman shuffles past, towing behind her a five-year-old boy with a wounded foot and a bandaged ankle. The child half moans, half chants as he limps along, but both ignore the MSF van. The soldiers maintain their customary Rwandan disciplined courtesy, a remarkable quality in a Third World army. The journalist asks Julie for her last name; she refuses. Her identity is revealed in this work, not in the accidental possession of a parent's surname. A self-conscious Bonnie Leyton hesitantly points her camera at an exhausted white-haired refugee. He stares vacantly at her until he realizes she poses no threat, and he is confident enough then to share his booming, contemptuous laughter with us and the village. His laughter seems to echo across the damp and cloud-shrouded hills.

We spend the night at yet another gracious colonial MSF compound, where MSF newcomers brace themselves to meet the increasing numbers of refugees. They work with a hurried break for one meal until they go to bed at midnight, and are up again at 4:30 the following morning. The tension mounts, the fear that the crisis may prove to be too much to handle. Eighteen medical and administrative people will be arriving here in the next twenty-four hours, and they will need food and mattresses, medical supplies, and instructions. The day after, nineteen more will arrive from France – nurses, a doctor, a water and sanitation man, a logistician, and an extra administrator – as MSF mobilizes fully for the emergency, dragging its European and Canadian volunteers out of their comfortable homes and on board any air transport they can commandeer. In the end, MSF International will have fielded 116 volunteers to meet the 1996 Rwandan emergency – 23 physicians, 26 nurses, 29 logisticians, 15 water and sanitation experts, 19 administrators, 2 psychologists, and 2 epidemiologists.

Monique reports the current best guess that a half-million "returnees" have already crossed the Zaire–Rwanda border and are heading south towards us along the narrow road. There are eighty-five reported cholera cases in the town of

Goma in Zaire, but none are yet known to have crossed the border into Rwanda. They remain in Zaire along with hundreds of thousands of other refugees who flee in every direction from the militias. Many wonder aloud if the returnees will bring the dreaded cholera with them, and if we are in for a repeat of 1994 – when in what has come to be called "The Judgement" for the nation's butchery, Rwandans began to sicken with cholera and to die.

～

The following morning, yet another apparently insane Rwandan driver races us back to Kigali, ignoring the thunderous downpour, his bald tires, and the windshield wipers, which have utterly ceased to function. We return to the capital to find the emergency team house in chaos. Six Belgian and French MSFers, two Scandinavians, and a Canadian have arrived from Europe, exhausted and frustrated. They had made their separate ways to Oslo the previous day, then flown all night from Norway on a Ukrainian-crewed Ilyushin transport plane, its immense cargo bay stuffed with aid supplies. On the airplane, they slept on a metre-deep bed of BP5 high-protein biscuits, and urinated in Coca-Cola bottles because no toilets were available for them. At a brief stopover in Cairo, they brazened their way past the protesting armed guards to get to the airport's toilets.

Here in Kigali, those who have worked together on previous postings at once recognize each other as somehow old

MSFers, summoned to meet the emergency, arrive in Kigali, Rwanda.

and dear friends. Amidst much hugging and squeals of delight, each immediately grabs a foam mat and creates a personal space on the floor, piling her possessions on the mattress and her gifts of European cheeses, breads, and salamis on the kitchen table. Those who know how to plan ahead will briefly scrub their bodies under a cold shower. Then together they boisterously depart for a restaurant meal on what will surely be their last free evening for many weeks. The next morning, some will notice that the bottom of the cheeses are writhing with maggots, their fecundity inspired by the African heat. A press officer laughs. They have a sharp and bitter taste, these maggots.

The medical matériel accumulates as quickly as the personnel. In MSF's main warehouse in Kigali, twenty thousand heavily guarded square feet of precious supplies are packed from floor to ceiling in preparation for the demands to come. There are oral-rehydration kits, medical bags, the universal BP5 high-protein biscuits, stretchers, surgical kits, all brought in from Europe on whatever plane is available – from commercial airlines to chartered former U.S.S.R. military jets – briefly to rest here among the scurrying rats. Chlorination kits, including water testers; U.S.A. refined vegetable oil; laundry soap from Uganda; kitchen sets from Dar es Salaam "Financed by the European Community Humanitarian Office for UNHRC"; "KliniDrapes" for private consultations; single-use medical gowns; and an entire room for medicines (mainly antibiotics) and medical equipment – including a stack of sphygmomanometers, the inevitable amputation kits with saw and scissors, laryngoscopes, stethoscopes, and weight scales. They will be used by MSF in the field, or given to other aid agencies when the need is great.

⌣

Until the well-publicized famine in Ethiopia, international medical aid was not well organized, even by MSF. Yet such a task is now understood to be relatively simple because the medical problems so engendered are inevitably standardized and easily anticipated. Thus, amputation, dehydration, dysentery, malaria, and cholera are all dealt with under MSF medical routines. Every station is provided with a medical kit that includes essential drugs for the usual range of disorders and a copy of the MSF guidelines. The manual reminds medical officers of appropriate procedures for an assessment of the situation and how best to estimate the number of dressings, rehydrates, and medicines that will be required for any threatened population. It also provides an *aide-mémoire* for simple surgery – from how to stitch a damaged eye to the best way to amputate a limb. Clamps and instruments are included in the kit to deal with the multitude of traumatic injuries encountered in isolated clinics, especially in war zones.

The essence of MSF work is emergency, crisis, temporary; and their "hospitals" are makeshift affairs at best. "Most of our work is short-term, and once a situation is stabilized we hand it on to other organizations," says one nurse. At Little Wall Camp on the Zairean border, an abandoned warehouse has been converted into a temporary MSF/Merlin hospital, its unpaved "floor" consisting of lumps of dusty volcanic rock, here and there awash in muddy puddles. Outside is the now-empty refugee camp: today, sixteen corpses are pulled from its tents. Inside the warehouse/hospital, we watch a young girl, her body wasted by unclean water and intolerable sanitary conditions, vomit onto a small table: the thin regurgitant is alive with parasitic worms. A young French physician in her filthy MSF vest carries a dead baby. She is followed by a bent and crippled man who supports his wife with one hand and cradles in his other arm an older child.

Fifty stretchers are arranged on top of once-white plastic pads, their inhabitants rehydrating with oral and intravenous salts, or gulping clean water from communal red plastic cups. Inevitably, the fine dust from the lava rock drifts onto the pads, just as the water spilled from drinking cups and the continuous spraying of chlorine disinfectant converts the dust to a light mud that is soon tracked onto the pads. An emaciated child contemplates empty space with that lost and broken stare of the wounded; farther down the aisle, a man has collapsed, falling on his back as if crucified on the ground. A half-dozen MSF medical workers and a dozen Red Cross Rwandans do their best to tend to the patients' needs. A second French M.D. moves from stretcher to stretcher, closely studying each patient before issuing instructions to his staff. The contact between the medical staff and their patients is electric, a melding of souls through eye and hand that MSFers themselves often describe as "emotional," or even "falling in love."

An assistant methodically walks up and down each aisle, spraying a cloud of disinfectant in front of him from a converted European garden-herbicide sprayer. A ten-year-old girl, abandoned by her parents, will not eat: an MSF press officer thinks the child "wishes to die," but coaxes her until she reluctantly takes a mouthful. Outside the hospital, the last of the thousands of refugees stream by. An extraordinarily muscular man passes with herculean strides, sweat pouring in rivers from his rippled body as with each step he heaves to push a homemade wheelbarrow balanced on one erratically wobbling wooden wheel. It is inconceivable that one man can move this barrow, stacked as it is to its gunwales with hundreds of kilos of furniture, food, wood, carpets, jerrycans of water.

Racing on his motorbike madly back and forth along the road from Gisenyi to Little Wall Camp to supervise the way stations is the Spanish M.D., Juan, performing one of the primary roles of MSF doctors: assessment, planning, coordination, determining which diseases are erupting, and designing their response. A few months later he will narrowly escape the massacre of his colleagues. For the moment, he threads his motorbike through the refugees in that Spanish driving style that blends gusto and finesse with pure insanity, endlessly tooting his horn as he forces a tiny space between people and vehicles. A press officer estimates MSF is giving

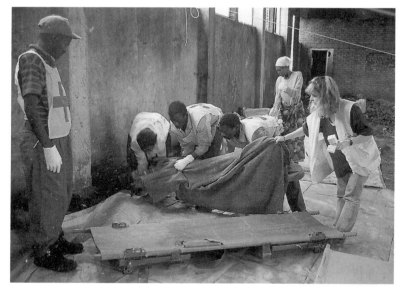

Above and opposite: Little Wall Camp, Gisenyi, Rwanda.

one thousand oral rehydrations and two hundred intravenous drips each day on this short stretch of road.

Over a hurried meal at the Gisenyi MSF house, Balzac, the radio operator, mentions with a false casualness that he has found the body of a dead eight-year-old boy just outside the compound. The local staff workers – Rwandan nationals – will not touch the child's remains, even with gloves, for they fear the presence of cholera. Logistician Franz struggles to keep the medical supplies moving despite his obvious exhaustion: "This morning I had to rush to unload twenty tons of supplies, and it's so important to keep them clean, it was just a nightmare."

A few moments later, Balzac rushes into the house to show us the live hand grenade (its pin in place) that has just been casually lobbed into the garden behind our tent, tossed on the fire as "a warning" of the Interhamwe's presence and malevolent intention. Simultaneously, a few kilometres away, a grenade is placed in front of each tire of Leslie's Toyota Land Cruiser. At precisely 11:09 A.M., anti-aircraft guns from a Zairean military base down the road open fire at an American reconnaissance plane that is circling the breathtaking beauty of Lake Kivu below our house. The firing continues sporadically all morning. "Oh shit," says a press officer, "next they'll be dropping the shells right here like they did last time in '94. They're only a few kilometres away. We had to evacuate then. Get out," she shouts to us. "It's time to get out."

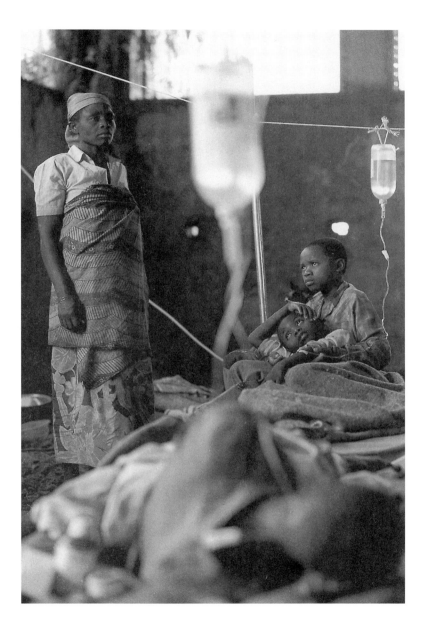

Hutu refugees and MSF staff at Little Wall Camp hospital.

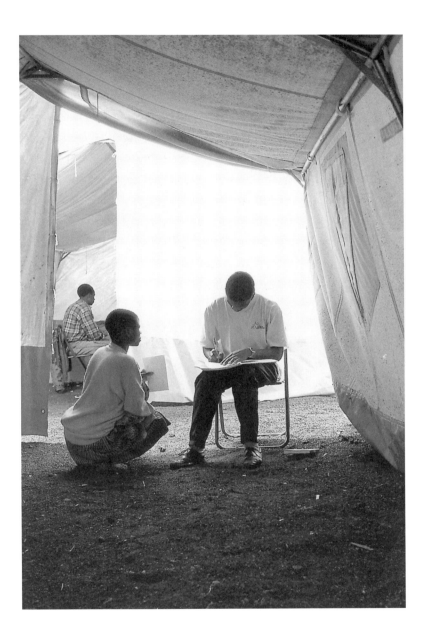

The Rwandan holocaust left ugly scars for life on the minds of some MSF surgeons, both witnesses to the horror and themselves victimized by the death squads. Some nights, the militias would creep into the hospital wards after all were asleep and hack to death the recovering maimed whose lives had been frantically saved scant hours before. Occasionally still, the surgeons sit bolt upright at night, awakened by silent screams. Cowering in fear in the hospital at night, the surviving patients in the adult wards would begin to sing together in the traditional Rwandan style. Soon they would be joined by the voices of the children from their own wards, a male nurse remembers. A rumour circulates that aid organizations trying to reunite separated families have had to change their strategy. Their method of circulating to the parents "head and shoulders" photographs of abandoned children has sown panic among the refugees: the parents, unaccustomed to seeing such pictures, assume they are being shown likenesses of their beheaded children.

MSF prefers emergency work, and does its best to pass long-term projects on to affiliated agencies. Today, MSF affiliates offer programs in medical education, and for the handicapped. In the Health Net hospital in the bombed-out slums of Kigali, they train Rwandan M.D.s in the techniques of emergency surgery so that cases in the countryside need not clog the cities' hospital facilities. They teach amputations to minimize the tissue loss from land mines' classic multiple injuries; the proper methods for dealing with bullet, machete, and shrapnel wounds; the nature of the complicated fractures from the traffic accidents that bedevil the Third World; and the special techniques for reamputation in order to fit an artificial prosthesis. On the table beside the lecturer is a plastic reproduction of an amputated limb: the lecturer is animated, and the young Rwandan M.D.s politely interrupt with many questions regarding the precise methods to be used.

↠

I spent my entire childhood living on the top floor of an isolated Saskatchewan rural hospital, where my father was the only doctor and coroner. I watched my first autopsy when I was five. Despite that early exposure and an entire career spent in the study of homicide, and despite a bogus veneer of toughness cultivated over a lifetime, I hurriedly leave the class, run behind the Health Net hospital, and vomit all my fear of Rwanda.

↠

An hour's drive southwest of Kigali, we visit the MSF-affiliated Belgian Catholic Brothers of Charity commune, the long-established health-care centre that has reopened after the massacres, rapes, mutilations, and sacking. Four or five aging Brothers from Belgium, one young Rwandan Brother, and a few volunteer teachers from Portugal and Switzerland run this orphanage, school, hospital, dispensary, and prosthesis factory. The factory trains most of Rwanda's laboratory assistants, who are themselves virtually all disabled. The malaria-ridden Brothers, happily isolated from the rest of the world all their adult lives, seem to have stepped out of the pages of Graham Greene's novel of back-country Zaire, *A Burnt-Out Case*, but the children (blind, deaf, deformed, land-mined, orphaned) seem healthy enough on their unappealing diet of sorghum gruel, and cheerful as they came out to greet us. In the heartbreakingly intimate greeting of the tiny Rwandan child, each in turn looks us in the eye, smiles, and then hugs our legs.

The day before we leave Rwanda, we visit an MSF-sponsored medical group that operates out of Butare's superb hospital near the dangerous Burundi border – "the cleanest and best equipped in Africa," boasts Carmen. Later, the charismatic Georg takes us to his cholera camp nearby, reminding us of the special problems medicine encounters in the heart of Central Africa. "Resistance to antibiotics is growing here in this situation – the classical [pharmaceutical] regime is no longer functional." In his camp, any "discharges" from the sick are the biggest problem: thus, all water and sewage from cholera patients must be rigidly controlled; and everyone entering or leaving the camp must have her hands washed and feet scrubbed with chlorine. Anyone coming from a cholera zone is immediately put in isolation, as is anyone who has the telltale diarrhea. As we walk along the only path to and from the camp, our boots sink deep into the camp's sewage. "Wash them well," Georg warns us.

Back in Kigali that evening, I summon all my resolve and try to clean our boots, but my revulsion overwhelms me. Stricken with shame, I offer our houseman, Fredo, all my remaining Rwandan money if only he will clean them for me. The following morning we escape from Rwanda, only to be shamed again. This time it is guilt by association, by a compatriot on the flight to Nairobi. We watch a boorish and loud-mouthed fellow Canadian, representing one of the evangelical Christian aid agencies, inexplicably stride up and down the airplane's aisle boasting to all who will listen, "I don't give a damn about Rwanda, I'm only in this for what I can get out of it."

Somalia

While we head to Nairobi, Kenya, our restless photographer Greg Locke cadges a ride on a UN flight to Dadaab, in Kenya near the Somali border. Here, 120,000 Somalis seek protection in what Locke calls "an established long-term project in a very hostile environment." The camp's inhabitants have fled from the predatory Somali warlords, the three-year drought, and the free-roaming drug dealers. The no-man's land in which they find a pathetic form of refuge is in theory "patrolled by a section of the Kenyan military," but in practice it is controlled by bandits who attack relief convoys, medical compounds, and refugee camps at will. In this way, "murder, rape, and theft are added to the misery of famine, drought, malnutrition, and disease," Locke notes. The MSF team sent in to the camps to cope with the outbreak of cholera consists of seven women and two men: a Bosnian M.D. as medical co-ordinator, a Swedish surgeon, two impossibly young Swedish physicians ("the baby doctors," we will always call them), one French and one Dutch doctor, two nurses, and a logistician/ administrator. Here, away from the international television cameras and the humanitarian agencies' internecine struggle for recognition and "air time," the medical workers can "go about their business with little of the fanfare and flag waving we saw in Rwanda," says Locke. "Here, they just get on with the job."

Each Dadaabian night there will be a fresh tragedy to mourn and share. "At night," Locke records, "the expatriate staff leave the camp hospital to seek security in their walled compound, leaving their patients in the hands of local staff – anyone with nursing training who can assist, or speak on the radio to the MSFers. A call comes in to the compound: 'Woman has given birth, but is very anaemic, heart rate and pulse down, needs blood transfusion.' The doctors scramble to give instructions over the radio to a local worker who has little medical training and barely speaks English. Ten minutes later, the worker calls back to say the woman has died, 'baby okay, is being nursed by its aunt.'" Six others die that night in the camp's hospitals.

After days of frustrating negotiation, Locke finally catches a flight – in a tiny bush plane smuggling a local drug into Kenya – to rejoin us in Nairobi. But he had arrived in Dadaab after the first rain had fallen in three years: the rains had flooded the concretized earth and unleashed a plague of anopheles mosquitoes, at least one of which bit into him and deposited its malarial protozoans in his bloodstream.[23]

MSF's head of mission in Somalia, Ian, is back in Nairobi after assessing a program designed to cope with the country's endemic tuberculosis. At the moment, only wealthy Somalis obtain proper treatment, and the remainder at best receive only a few weeks' medication, which if anything is worse than useless. "It's primarily a TB project, but it looks as if we'll also give assistance to a general hospital that is already there because their staff don't have much training and they're short of supplies. The way I'm going to do it is to start with an initial phase of six months in the hospital to give them a feel for who we are. They have so little access to funds, so we'll help them build up a small TB program that has already been started. The sustainability of a lot of Somali programs has been a problem: previous programs have just disappeared when the aid agencies left. I'm working now with a Somali doctor who's been practising medicine there for thirty-five years. When he tells me something about Somalia, I listen."

Kenya

Kenya's capital, Nairobi, is the East African headquarters for all the national MSF sections operating in the area. At a crossroads in the centre of Nairobi, a rat stands nonchalantly behind a ragged man who lives on the scraps and garbage he has piled beneath the traffic light. On the path to MSF's Kabira clinic in the wretched slums of the city, a young man with a withered leg sprawls at a corner to practise his brand of penny capitalism. The goods he offers for sale – secondhand shoes and plastic dishes – are spread out on blankets before him to give them a measure of protection from the ever-intrusive flowing mud. He ignores the periodic rainshowers and sits motionless: so long as he does not move, the mud will not rise above the blanket.

Posters decorate the Kabira clinic wall. Appropriate paintings underline the printed messages: a child is defecating and eating in the same spot, a man makes unprotected love to several women in turn.

THE FOUR Fs — FAECES, FOOD, FINGERS, FLIES.
YOUR WIFE AND CHILDREN NEED YOU — PROTECT
YOUR FAMILY, USE A CONDOM.
HASSAN IS SICK — HE NEVER USES THE LATRINE.

What has to be taught in the slums is depressingly simple, but it is still improbable western theory to much of the Third World – don't eat where you shit, wash your hands after a bowel movement, avoid unprotected sex. In the clinic's two consulting rooms, two nurses and a half-dozen assistants offer the slum's residents their only affordable medical care. Children play on the muddy road outside, while on six days of each week inside the clinic the nurses deal with forty to fifty cases of malaria, respiratory and skin infections, sexually transmitted diseases, and whatever else is brought to them. Difficult cases are referred to the government-subsidized national hospitals, which prescribe free drugs that have been donated to them by MSF.

In front of a small admitting desk in the clinic stands a woman with her sick child: she presents her Kenyan national immunization card for tuberculosis, diphtheria, polio, tetanus, whooping cough, and measles to show she's been here before. "This is one of our efforts," says one of the nurses, Sylvia, "to encourage people to come for immunization." Unfortunately, "they usually bring the child the first time, but they don't take it seriously, and they forget about it when they move from the Nairobi slums and return to their rural homes."

Amin, the elegant ethnic-Somali nurse, notes that "most of the patients here must be dewormed. They have worms because of the food they eat." She shows me the daily patient log for the clinic: "Diagnoses for 11 November 1996 – 13 cases of malaria, one mastitis, two pneumonia, one of peptic ulcers and one amoebic dysentery. We give Chloroquin for malaria, an antibiotic for pneumonia, Metrondizole for amoebic dysentery. If they were untreated, three out of ten with malaria will die." Patients with intractable problems, such as cancer, are sent straight to the hospital.

An MSF agronomist is convinced that in Africa the biggest problem for the future is not "traditional disease," but AIDS. "We know that so many children become orphans from AIDS, and it has a lot of social impact because nobody is taking care of them. The AIDS orphans stay with a sick relative, one-third of whom are from [poverty-stricken] West Kenya. Thus, income is even further reduced in the family. They go on the streets – they beg, steal, sniff glue, and get into child prostitution. They are physically weak and are sexually molested by grown-ups; and then they get AIDS themselves." Naturally, she finds it "depressing when we see such young patients *and* their babies with AIDS." Even worse is the ignorance. "I think over 90 per cent of people have *heard* of AIDS," but she and her colleagues find it difficult to convince their patients that AIDS has anything to do with unprotected sex. Because the population is already weakened by malnutrition and disease, "the life expectancy with HIV here in the slums is *two years*, not ten to fifteen years as in the West." More ominously, "research here suggests 25 per cent of all deaths are AIDS related," with much more to come.

She adds that cultural notions of shame regarding AIDS further inhibits the possibility of treatment. "People whisper about AIDS because they associate it with promiscuity and prostitution – so you are stigmatized. They have not portrayed a positive image here. Here in Kenya, AIDS is *hidden*. We have private hospitals that want to keep their image and make money, so they don't declare they have AIDS patients at all." Such local sensitivities often prevent AIDS even from being recorded as the official cause of death. "We also see a lot of malaria. People move into the slums from the rural areas and bring it with them. The city's poor sewage system [non-existent in the slum] assists the spread."

Amin is twenty-four, twelve years younger than her

mother. Other staff tease Amin that she herself is the mother of several half-grown children, at home with their father in the north. She tries to "teach people there are alternatives to prostitution as they come into the 50,000-plus shantytown here. Teaching them about sanitation, condoms, alternatives to prostitution such as making charcoal, working as a house-maid, as a day labourer, or just selling vegetables in the market." She thinks "it's the ignorance of the rural popula-tion" that lets these diseases spread. "I deal with adults – nine adults this morning. The problems were upper-respiratory tract infections, and malaria – yes, I have had malaria myself several times. There were nine of us at home, my brothers and sisters, and now we are five – four died. My brother just died of typhoid at twenty-seven, I just came from his funeral. Two sisters and one brother died as babies. We don't have clean water, so it carries typhoid, we bring it from the river. Part of the town has clean water, but the clean water tank only ser-vices the old inner town. A bigger water tank would end typhoid in our village. Here in the slum they get clean water from pipes. The problem here is the latrines."

In the consultation room, Amin coaxes a medical history from a young man, then takes his temperature, inserting a sterilized thermometer under his arm. She measures his heartbeat with a stethoscope and gives him a prescription. Two more men arrive for a medical review, one recovering from malaria, the other with high blood pressure. Soon there is a whole group outside, two women with sick children, and two teenagers. The children are weighed and measured, their temperature taken, and medicines dispensed where necessary. In the tiny clinic "garden" that afternoon, the MSF nurses give an advanced class in midwifery to five working African midwives.

Ebullient Rose studied nursing in a mission hospital. Like so many in the Third World, her father was struck by an automobile and died when she was very young, and "my mother was helped by the mission." After she qualified in nursing, she "worked in a private hospital for four years, then I joined MSF. I had two brothers, but one died – he was knocked down by a car, too, twenty-five years old and married with four children. I have five sisters, all alive. I think they should give money to this slum because sanitation is so bad and once someone is infected with an illness it spreads so fast. They pass diarrhea everywhere because they have no toilets. Pneumonia will spread, most people here are poor, so they can't go to private hospitals and we find they are dying from it."

Back at MSF (Holland) headquarters in Nairobi, Priscilla, the country medical coordinator, says over breakfast that she awaits news from the Northern Kenyan MSF teams about the reported "dramatic" increase in mortality rates from diarrhea in the drought-ridden northern desert country. Dutch nurse Selina is checking their supply of children's anti-malarial syrup, which appears to be ineffectual and may have been damaged by extended storage in overheated warehouses. Martha, an American nurse, is involved in an immunization project in the Sudan. She says there has been no health care of any kind there for two years, so people have had no immunization – and they are stricken with polio, measles, tetanus, malaria (the number-one killer), respiratory diseases (number two), and diarrhea (the third most prolific killer). Three-quarters of that Sudanese population are Dinka pastoralists; among whom a cow is more "respected" than a person (indeed, Vétérinaires Sans Frontières were more enthusiastically welcomed than MSF, she adds, because if their cows die then so does all the family).

⌒

At MSF (Holland) headquarters for East African operations, Morris – the introspective English country manager for Kenya – broods over the larger issues of medical practice and public health. Sitting in his handsome office overlooking the gardens of Nairobi, he emphasizes the essentially *political* origins and consequences of "humanitarian" crises. His primary concern is "the social deterioration that comes with a long, aggressive war. Sudan, for example, has been at war for thirty or forty years: civil society is destroyed, and what remains are the predatory systems for those with guns. The public health aspects of civil war – disease, devastation, destruction – all break down.

"How can we even guess what our impact on this might be?" Morris asks. "At the individual level we can use crude health statistics – we treat thirteen hundred people a week in South Sudan who would otherwise have had no health care. So that's a figure, thirteen hundred who have walked long distances – as far as a hundred kilometres – many of whom might otherwise have died. So at this level, you can say, 'Well, we have spent this much money and done this and saved their lives and stopped them from infecting others.'

"But you can't judge such matters simply on 'cost effectiveness' and numbers of patients. In an acute emergency you have to focus on the potential adult survivors – their labour and their health are the main sources of the group's capacity to survive. Then you have to look at how we are increasing the productivity of individuals (men have to clear a field: if a man gets malaria, his family will starve because his labour is absolutely critical to the survival of his whole family). Who else does a community depend upon the most? The sand fly, which carries the dreadful wasting disease, Kala-Azar, bites at dawn and at dusk – just when cattle herders walk into their villages, so it's the herders who get bitten and get Kala-Azar. It's similar to a war where most males are taken away to fight and the whole food production system suddenly is dropped onto the young females."

Moreover, Morris wonders, which community should we encourage and strengthen, the refugee camp or their original home? Our current project in the Sudan is in a camp where refugees have been living for five years, under circumstances in which their survival capacity is seriously reduced. "Yet if it's bad in the areas where they came from, that's where the effort should be, not in the refugee camps – so if and when they do eventually return to their homes they'll be capable of recolonizing their own land; fixing their homes, wells, and fields," explains Morris. "It's a risky strategy because the area might be attacked again: they have to make the decision about when to return, and we have to make the right decision about what to support with limited resources – only then is it a positive contribution." The discussions and arguments go on endlessly. Inescapably, there is much more to medicine than the practice of medicine.

Heavy rains flood the camp on the Somalia–Kenya border.

Album: On the Border

The MSF specialist in the construction of cholera camps goes to work.

Patient being wheeled into Ifo camp hospital, Dadaab.

Somali cholera victims, Dadaab.

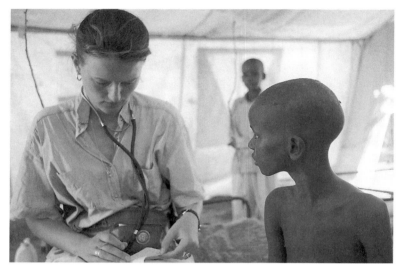

French MSF doctor and Somali refugee suffering from tuberculosis.

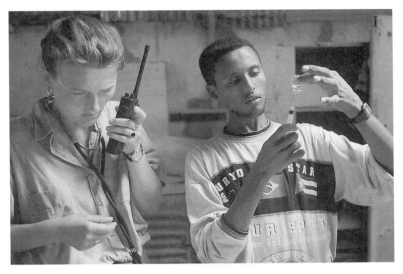

Doctor and Somali assistant at Ifo camp hospital, Dadaab.

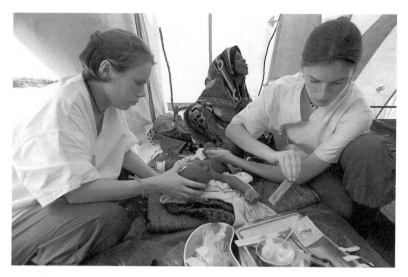

MSF doctors and Somali child, Dadaab.

Tuberculosis victim, Dagehalla refugee camp, Dadaab.

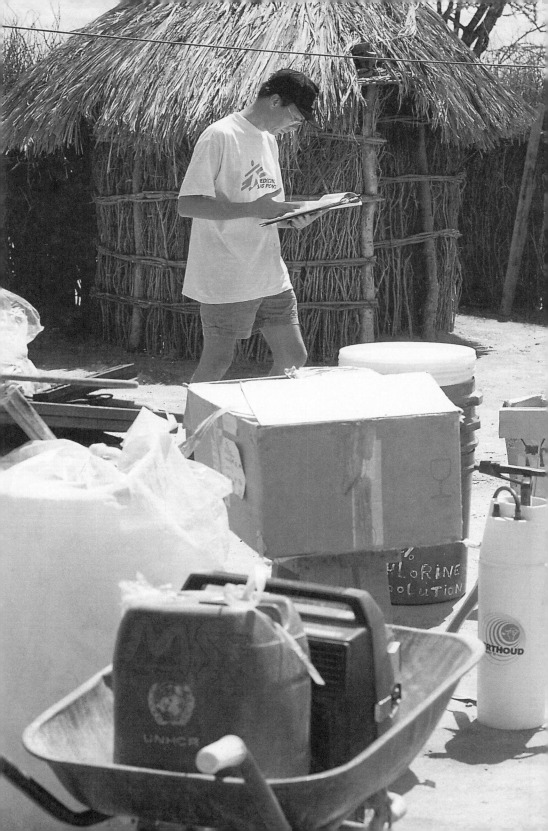

4

Brainstorming, Briefings,

and Round Tables

"M<small>SF</small> is not a bureaucratic, top-down organization like the civil service or the CBC, *it's flat*," says a senior press officer who, like so many other salespersons, mistakes appearance for reality. Yet what else could it be but egalitarian – at least in theory – with a medical staff of such prestigious physicians and nurses being ordered about by administrators, transport managers, accountants, and logisticians? Indeed, with its brushing aside of conventional status distinctions and its consistent use of opinions from workers in "the field," the organization does struggle to be a consensual one. After the massacre of Spanish doctors in Ruhengeri, MSFers were asked to vote whether they should

Opposite: Setting up a cholera hospital in Dadaab.

stay or leave: they voted to stay, but those who did not feel comfortable with the decision were free to leave.

Nevertheless, despite the non-hierarchical style and the vivid protestations, ultimately MSF is top-down. It has to be. When Patrick was Burundi's country manager, one of his most urgent and recurring staff problems was that "some of them are crazy!" Perhaps his most troublesome task was when he was forced to relieve from duty one MSF doctor who had worked in a village for months, making friends and saving lives – "falling in love with them," as the French MSFers sometimes describe this encounter with the people they serve. When the physician learned that "enemy" troops were headed their way to stage a massacre, he somehow found a flak jacket and an AK-47 assault rifle and ran "to save" the village. He cut a ridiculous figure clad in his shorts and sandals, but, more importantly, he violated the prime mandates of MSF – thou shalt neither take sides nor bear weapons. "Okay," shouted Patrick, "you're out of here!" The astonished M.D. protested, "But this is not the army; this is not a hierarchy. Let's negotiate!" "Surprise!" said Patrick. "This *is* a hierarchy and I'm in charge. You're out on the next plane." It must be this way or many will die, and the ethical credibility of MSF will be squandered.

Inevitably then, MSF is run along military lines, not according to some egalitarian mystique: after all, relief workers routinely go alone and unarmed to ferociously dangerous places. Indeed, journalist Robert Kaplan writes, they consistently "put up with far worse conditions and in many cases more physical danger, than do increasingly pampered Western troops, whom the Western public and politicians are more and more reluctant to expose to real physical risk." Unlike modern governments, MSF delights in risk-taking. Not for nothing do MSF offices sometimes resemble a military camp, replete with door signs written in Mil Spec (military specification) English – WAT-SAN, COM, LOG & OPS, MED, ADMIN – as in any military base. More and more, relief workers go where the military fears to tread, and from Chechnya to Rwanda take hostile fire that once was aimed at armies.[24]

To navigate this complex minefield of safety requirements, ideological coherence, and wounded feelings, MSF procedures feature daily briefings from heads of missions (SITREPS, situation reports, in the allegedly non-military, non-hierarchical organizational language), heated all-night brainstorming sessions to debate new dilemmas, and on-the-spot "round-table" discussions to discuss evolving situations.

Emergency Briefings

In emergencies such as Rwanda's in late 1996, with the racist killings again beginning to mount, each worker's attention is riveted on the morning's briefing at MSF headquarters in Kigali. It is 8 A.M., Saturday, November 23, 1996. This morning's briefing follows hard upon an all-night brainstorming session in which most staffers participated. The head of mission and the country's medical coordinator gather thirty expatriate staff members behind the aristocratic home that is now their central station. Seated at outdoor tables in front of a chalkboard, the doctors, nurses, epidemiologists, water and sanitation specialists, logisticians, and radio operators listen raptly to the reports and the assessment. By the time they begin to disperse in the late morning, their lives may depend on the quality of information they have received and absorbed.

No one stirs as the abrupt and businesslike station head, Maria, points to the map and recounts that over the weekend an estimated 350,000 refugees have just crossed the border from Zaire into Rwanda to end their two-year exile. The first to return appeared to be in good health, stopping at each United Nations or Red Cross transit camp for water or biscuits before continuing on their march; and they were not harassed (or even searched for weapons) by government troops. Yesterday, however, the government had decided that the refugees must move at a faster pace to clear the roads for possible military operations.

Conclusion: The urgent requirements are first water, then food. All along the dozens of kilometres to Kigali, MSF has virtually overnight established water stations every few kilometres, offering latrines, rehydration, and access to basic medical care. This is an astonishing achievement, and it required impeccable planning and the flawless coordination of the dozens of freshly arrived MSF expatriates, as well as the efforts of other aid agencies. Sites had to be selected; water bladders ordered, delivered, and connected; latrines dug; tents erected; medicines delivered; medical staff placed. And when the refugees have passed these stations, the facilities must be ripped up and replanted farther along the routes. The primary fear is of a cholera outbreak, which could kill thousands as it did in 1994. The reality is that many are severely dehydrated and in danger of dying.

Yet the government is now anxious to clear the highway quickly, says Maria, and it has therefore decided that no food other than the bare minimum necessary to sustain life should be distributed until the refugees have returned to their own communes. "So our relationship with the government is deteriorating, and they are closing our water stations." There are still many people on the road: right now there are perhaps ten thousand between the way stations from Goma to Ruhengeri, where the authorities are putting them on buses. There are thirty to forty thousand more on the road south to Kigali; another ten thousand heading east; five thousand south of Mukungwa; and small numbers headed in all directions.

"To facilitate communication with the government, that is, to make it appear as if we are accommodating their needs when we are not precisely doing so, we have changed the names of our centres. We don't call them way stations any more, we call them health posts," Maria explained. "This makes the government happier because it sounds as if the refugees are just stopping briefly with us. So now we also have rest points, with a few patients. In addition, we are moving along the road with the refugees. There are six MSF tents at Ruhengeri hospital. So, our operational plan is organized as follows:

"First Step – Emergency on the Road: Our health posts and rest points are now well established.

"Second Step – Action in the Communes: Once the refugees return to their homes, we have to make sure there are no major health problems. So mobile teams in vans all over the area will try to get in and assess the work that will be needed in the communes."

Ivan, a Danish physician, interrupts with a question: "You are not moving cholera patients, are you?" "No," Maria replies. "We are moving the vulnerables, and the refugees where we can, in trucks, vans, and minibuses. We have found no solution yet for the vulnerables, people who can't go on any longer. We assist them with moving in trucks to the rest points, we give them food and water, and then keep them moving because the government doesn't want the roads clogged. This is a big frustration for everybody, and all other organizations are having the same problem with the vulnerables. Maybe we will have to accept it – we keep them moving and just do our best to make people a bit more comfortable.

"We had to stop giving out food earlier because we had riots when the crowds fought to get the food," she continues. "But now, with the refugees dispersed along the road, we can give them food. Our biscuit-distribution system works fine at fixed points every ten kilometres after Ruhengeri. Once the refugees are back in their communes – and remember that there are three hundred communes in Rwanda – they will be given food and water, and then registered with the

Hutu refugee, Ruhengeri, Rwanda.

government. After that they will be given enough food to last them for six weeks.

"We had a brainstorming session last night to try to organize some kind of mobile food and water distribution, but we decided it is too dangerous, as people will rush into the traffic and get hurt. Last Friday when people arrived, they hadn't had food for five days. Now, the most vulnerable are still struggling, strung out along the road between Gisenyi and Ruhengeri."

Ivan asks about the availability of water after the refugees have passed through Ruhengeri. Maria replies that MSF has no legal right to intervene once the refugees have entered Kigali prefecture (an enormous administrative unit that surrounds the capital city). The government does not want MSF operating in Kigali: "Our mandate is not there." She adds that what the government does want is transit camps; and "what we want from you MSFers now is flexibility, do what we ask of you: 40 per cent of the problem now is diarrhea, and all went well yesterday without any problems."

Maria continues: "Third Step: Revenge killings and disputes over property are inevitable once people have returned to the communes. You'll be the people closest to them, we need your *witnessing*. We have a responsibility for human rights," to tell the world what is going on.

"Intelligence Report: U.S. satellite photos have found two groups of refugees, one hundred thousand and another of one hundred and fifty thousand, moving *away* from Rwanda in a northwesterly direction, but we have no information yet on the rest of Zaire."

Maria turns her attention to individuals. "Duties: Now, who's going where? Alexandro, you're going to Gisenyi, there are eighty thousand refugees in the area. You two are going to Ruhengeri. Medical people and logisticians should stay behind now for the cholera update.

"Security: No travelling at night after dark. You new arrivals, don't forget that's after six o'clock here at the equator. Don't drive your own car – use a driver, he knows the conditions. There are more and more checkpoints. Always have the driver negotiate with the military. At checkpoints at night, stop the car and turn off the lights, turn on the inside light and open your window. Don't let the atmosphere get heated, turn the conversation away from politics and on to health subjects. Let them search if they want. *Never* bribe the military here. About team life: Don't forget you are suddenly arriving, try to avoid tensions. There are condoms everywhere, just help yourself. Try to sleep well."

Maria then introduces Wim, the epidemiologist who will give the public health report – focusing especially on the threat of cholera. Wim steps to the chalkboard and begins his preliminary scientific statement, based on days of studiously monitoring the refugees. "In terms of cholera, bring your own food and water to avoid any personal exposure. There are not many very severe patients. My hypothesis is that everybody in Goma's refugee camps was infected with cholera, but only 10 per cent actually got it, so they appear to have developed some kind of unprecedented partial immunity. Now, thanks to the water and san people, the water supply is good for the people on the road. The highest priority is access to oral rehydration, the cup out of a bucket. Second priority is to have teams going out and finding the sick people, picking them up and bringing them to the closest hospital or rehydration centre. There is a big problem of hygiene. There are still no latrines on the road, so the refugee's clothes are completely soiled. Therefore, our chlorine solution must be sprayed everywhere, on bodies and on clothes – that's more the logisticians than the nurses doing that, of course.

"If our hypothesis of partial immunity for returnees from the camps in Zaire is correct, it is still not true for those who never left Rwanda; so there might be a secondary spread of the disease when the refugees return to their communes," Wim continues. "We should have a strategy of making sure oral rehydration is also available in the communes – if so, we will have very few deaths. Antibiotics are not necessary, and it takes our attention away from rehydration." Singly and in pairs, they begin to disperse to their work, their drivers rushing them to their posts throughout Rwanda. A few physicians with further questions cluster around the epidemiologist.

Emergency Round Tables

Staffers can call a "round table" anywhere and at any time, bringing together for an instant meeting all those who might be affected by any issue, trivial or profound. We sat in on a number of such discussions in Rwanda and Kenya.

N. W. Rwanda, Ruhengeri Station, November 16, 1996, 6:10 P.M.: This is the day the refugees have begun to flood across the Zaire–Rwanda border. It is only a day or two's hard walk from there to Ruhengeri station, and the three MSFers there – a nutritionist turned station administrator, a water and sanitation engineer, and a nurse – brace for what is to come. Clive has spent the morning frantically locating the inexplicably missing couplings that connect the taps to the water bladders. Without them, many refugees will die of thirst. "It sounds stupid," he says, "but it's the kind of problem we're always having."

The three depart for a meeting with local UN representatives and other aid agencies to coordinate their plans for the next few days. They return at 8:30 P.M. and talk shop throughout the meal that we have prepared and served them. Clive asks anxiously about tomorrow's expected flood of more than a hundred thousand refugees. "So, you think three way stations are enough?" Monique, as always, moves to calm him: "It will be fine – provided there are enough UN water trucks tomorrow." They pore over tomorrow's plans until midnight, searching for flaws and omissions in their planning, damning other aid agencies for their inefficiencies, praising themselves. They are exhausted when they finally break, but Sylvia has another hour's work to do – reports to write and file on her computer, others to transmit by radio to Kigali. Clive will try to grab a shower, but we hear him yelp when the bitterly cold water hits his head. A few hours' sleep, and they will all be awake at five in the morning to make ready for their confrontation with the moving wave of refugees – who will have spent the night sleeping unprotected on the side of the road.

Kigali, Emergency Team House, November 21, 11:14 A.M.: Over the static on the radio, we hear: "Ronald, I have an urgent message from Balzac in Gisenyi – bombshells are going off." A hurried round table is formed: What to do about this freshened artillery barrage. Is this the long-dreaded first phase in the Interhamwe militia's attempt to retake Rwanda, starting with Goma's airport a few kilometres outside Rwanda's border? Decision: Wait and watch to see if it intensifies. It does not, but the shooting continues.

Kigali Slums: Expatriate Dutch nurse Wilhelmina, the head of mission of an MSF affiliate, must decide whether her organization should change its direction. The fierce philosophical argument with her senior national nurse, Anna, takes place in the back of a car hurtling along Rwanda's southwestern highway, its engine shrieking at its red line and scattering pedestrians in all directions. Indifferent to the likelihood we will all soon tumble off a cliff, they debate whether aid programs ultimately do any good at all. Anna, recently returned to Rwanda from the Tutsi diaspora in Uganda, believes passionately that they can do much good, especially in a bankrupt and demoralized nation such as Rwanda. Wilhelmina, perhaps jaded after years in development, thinks that aid can do good, but not much. They argue about how best to proceed with their programs, and how paternalistic their teaching must be. Anna believes their programs must *teach* people the "right way" to do things, such as ensuring a constant supply of clean water. Wilhelmina insists it is part of a "colonial mentality" to "tell" people what they want: what they want must come from them. The debate, and the round tables, will continue whenever they consider launching a new program or pause to reassess.

Stable Operations

In stable operations, where MSF workers are not immediately threatened by catastrophe, the atmosphere at a meeting can be more genteel – even banal – and the conversation a mix of the fundamental and the trivial, the latter apparently designed primarily to relieve petty irritation.

Nairobi, Kenya, "The White House," MSF (Holland) East African Headquarters, November 27, 9:30 A.M.: Daily meeting in the "boardroom," with six MSFers present. Dutch nurse Selina, training to be a country manager, opens the meeting with a question: "So, the plane is going to Rwanda with Robert's coat?" Vague murmurs indicate that yes, Robert's forgotten coat is being brought to him. Priscilla, the country's medical coordinator, asks, "Anything on the radio?" "No messages – except Sudan's order for weight scales and food," says Japp, their financial officer. Logistician John adds that "Johann and Völker are coming down from Sudan on a flight – they are running out of food." Later, we learn from Völker that for weeks they have been living entirely on the only foodstuff left in the camp, the widely loathed tinned corned beef.

Priscilla turns the brief meeting to serious items. "These Sudanese TB patients are very sick, and they're malnourished – the UN is primarily responsible. I'll talk to them on the highest levels to get them moving on this. Anything else?" They speak of ransacking one budget item to get money for another. "Shall we make the contract for these two new doctors the same? Or one for five months and one for seven months?" Financier Japp pleads, "Make it five for both, so the budget is the same." It is done. Priscilla asks, "Any other movement stuff? Anyone coming into Nairobi?" Japp answers, "No, but would it be possible to get information on upcoming R&Rs?" He is informed who is eligible for recreational leave. No one is claiming emergency evacuation, a right available to any MSFer at any time, with no questions asked. "Any other business?" asks Priscilla. "Could we change today's [budget] meeting to tomorrow?" "Tomorrow at 11 A.M. Any other points that need following up?" Japp asks for "a car for two or three hours" to check out a proposed MSF building rental. "That's it?" Priscilla asks. "Great," concludes Japp.

Nairobi, "The White House," December 2, 9:30 A.M., Morning Operations Meeting: Morris, the country manager, notes an "interesting report on the Sudan in the MSF *Newsletter*. I talked to Jeb in Sudan last night and they're running out of antibiotics – [but] to give them more drugs, we need to see the number of patients they're handling. Should we wait until the program is better set up before we send more?" Völker insists, "We should wait until we get the numbers" – to determine how much medicine has been given to how many patients – "otherwise they'll want stuff whenever they ask for it, without numbers." Priscilla agrees. "Let's set up a morbidity and mortality data centre before we send any drugs," she suggests. "I have a feeling they're providing more clinics than we approved – I think that's the issue. They may also be over-prescribing antibiotics: the medical assistants could be retrained."

Morris asks for an "update on all the programs," makes plans for visits to the major East African stations, and begins to shuffle staff around Kenya, Somalia, and Sudan – some staff need rest, some need new placements. "Antoinette needs to go to Holland on Friday. Jonathan needs to come out for R&R. Is there a plane?" Logistician John replies, "We've had to move quite a lot of TB patients. I have three air bookings just in case; and we still have three people coming on Sunday.

We could send them by road. Catherine will have to leave. Her father is in a coma in Holland and his brain functions are now dead. Send Humphrey in to cover for her?" Japp notes that Humphrey is "on holiday until Christmas." They find someone else, and the matter is resolved.

National Meetings

Finally, there are annual national and international meetings where problems of mutual concern can be discussed at length. November 1996's first annual Canadian meeting in Toronto brings together some fifty present and past members to share their concerns. There are more women than men in the room, and most are much younger than forty. There are a half-dozen brief and informal talks. A speaker in the afternoon urges them to re-examine their real impact on the societies they try to help: "Are we *actually* reducing mortality and morbidity rates? Are we *really* making a difference? We should always be evaluating ourselves." Another speaker wonders how clear they are about the long-term consequences of their actions: "How much do we destabilize? How much do we stabilize a country just by being there? What negative impact do we have on the people we help? How do we evaluate this?" However, when she asks for a routine program of self-evaluation, there is widespread indifference in the room (one man has already fallen asleep). Perhaps it smacks too much of conventional bureaucracy, of forms to be filled out and reports to be written, half the reasons they periodically abandon conventional life.

What are our true goals, asks a logistician? For that matter, how do we even define a humanitarian emergency? If it is an infrastructural collapse leaving whole populations without access to food, shelter, water, or access to medical care, what are our duties in such a crisis? To act as witnesses, and to provide a temporary infrastructure? MSFers can be argumentative, and they are filled with soul-searching questions. One demands to know why we use the misleading phrase "humanitarian emergency" at all when these are always *political* emergencies – a politically orchestrated genocide or famine that leads to a medical emergency? Moreover, what do we leave behind when we depart? Can our hosts really build on what we have done, or do our efforts disappear when we leave?

The personalities can also be as pugnacious and superficial as those in any academic or political gathering. One woman loudly and pointlessly complains that "some" MSFers hire prostitutes when abroad, but her comments are ignored. A pudgy MSF bureaucrat, flaunting his authority over us, does his best to insult us. A less-than-effervescent emissary from the Dutch parent office catches himself in mid-drone, finally notices the dozing MSFer, and asks, "Am I *that* boring?" Yet there is also a different emotional and intellectual texture, a shared set of understandings about their common adventure.

If employees in a conventional bureaucracy are merely rivals and enemies disputing possession of a limited resource, MSFers have little such rank to envy. Embedded in their mystique is a common obsession that marginalizes such competition.

Album: Clinic in the Slums

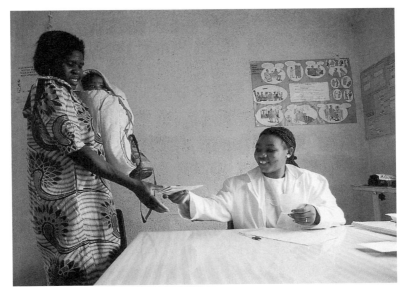

MSF clinic in Nairobi, Kenya.

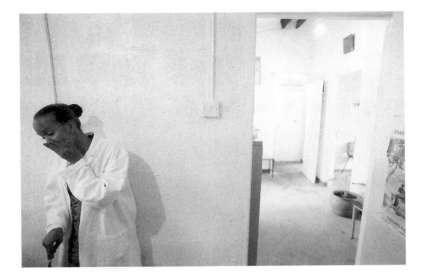

Ethnic Somali nurse with the ledger of patients seen.

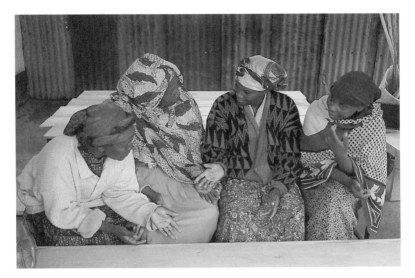

Midwives gather at MSF clinic, Nairobi.

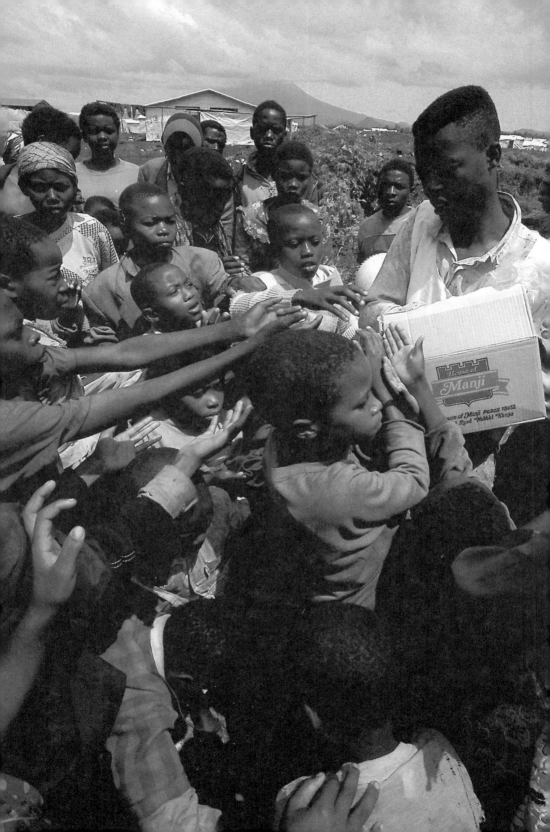

5

MSF and Its Critics

*T*he humanitarian industry's harshest critics – many of whom are MSF intellectuals – often express the view that the underlying political function for humanitarian aid is to serve as a kind of media-hyped smoke-screen to cover the political manipulations of the First World. This opaque atmosphere allows the governments of wealthy industrial nations to give the impression that they are struggling to help the disordered Third World when in fact they are doing very little. Indeed, the "aid" masquerade allows the imperial nations such as France and the United States to manipulate the impoverished world for their own geopolitical ambitions – under the cover of the alleged civilizing virtues,

Opposite: Aid worker distributes food to Hutu refugees, Gisenyi, Rwanda.

for example, of Francophonie or "Freedom." Further, it allows these governments to maintain a humanitarian image while their manufacturers are reaping enormous dividends. After all, the Third World is one of the primary customers for the five-hundred-billion-dollar annual arms trade; and its demand seems insatiable for all the hardware of modern war – for land mines, poison gas, small arms, artillery, tanks, and airplanes.

Many of the elite aid agencies – including MSF, Oxfam, and the International Committee of the Red Cross – do their best to distance themselves from such a squalid political economy. Yet if MSF is to maintain both its sense of purpose and its public credibility, its members must forever pick their way through a minefield of dilemmas and contradictions, ambiguities, political manoeuvring, and corrupting influences. Moreover, it must do so against a background of international ignorance about the plight of the Third World – a catastrophic poverty that the developed world, in its relentless pursuit of imperial grandeur, helped to create and maintain.

At the same time, the world's honeymoon with aid – contracted in the devastation that accompanied the Second World War and maintained by the rivalries between the super-powers during the Cold War – can now be re-invigorated only by media-friendly catastrophes. Thus, the developed world's overall aid budget shrank by nearly 10 per cent in the mid-1990s (relative to the size of its economy, Canada ranks sixth in the world in aid spending), while the expenditure on the more televisable emergency relief has quadrupled – to over

$8 billion. As the number of emergency-relief agencies multiplies, there is a mounting dependence on both public and private donations: the resulting circus that must capture their attention on television creates serious ethical problems, which one critic has glossed as the "counterfeiting of humanitarianism."

A major problem facing MSF is that it wishes to preserve its independence of thought and action, yet its activities must obviously be paid for – most often by imperial governments that have their own political agendas. Fund-raising is the trickiest of all activities, and one misstep can bring disaster. If MSF turns for financial help to government, then it must risk attempts to interfere with its independence. Should it choose to keep its distance from government and depend upon contributions from private donors, then it must turn to the monstrosity that is the public marketplace – and subordinate itself to the compromising demands of the media. Whichever path it chooses will surely be an ambiguous one. In practice, each national MSF section selects its own path. Some, such as France and the Netherlands, solicit private donations to balance their dependence on funding from national governments and the European Community. Others, such as Canada and Belgium, depend overwhelmingly on government grants (see Appendix).

A second major issue concerns the impossibility of fully anticipating the consequences of its actions in such complex and foreign political situations. To do nothing until such matters are fully understood would negate the very essence of

MSF – *immediate* emergency medical relief for endangered populations. Yet assistance to such populations is used by the warlords who commonly control the refugee camps: the warlords use the refugees to extort food and medicine from the aid agencies; and they use the aid workers as *de facto* emissaries from the First World recognizing the warlord's political legitimacy. Moreover, keeping the refugees herded together in camps in order to receive medicine, food, and water provides the warlords with a useful human shield against their equally predatory rivals. Thus, the decision to withhold assistance and see refugees suffer, or give aid and in doing so assist a murderous warlord, is by no means a simple one.

Finally, there is a fundamental question: Does aid actually do any good and, if so, how much? How do we even begin to assess the value of such work? The fact is that no one truly knows how to determine the value of aid; nor is it easy to justify helping a few hundred thousand victims when so many millions suffer on the planet. Just as MSF must delicately balance these conflicting mandates, so each worker must assess and resolve the dilemmas for herself.

Canada – like Australia, Japan, Denmark, the U.K., and the U.S.A. – is merely a "delegate office" supported by Canada's CIDA and the Netherlands' financial generosity, and responsible primarily for the mundane matters of staff recruitment, public relations, and supplementary funding. Some Canadian members are anxious to be more than merely a heavily subsidized satellite of the cautious and technocratic Dutch office, to make Canada an equal partner with

Children gather behind hospital, Gisenyi, Rwanda.
Overleaf: Displaced Zairean refugees, Lake Kivu, Sakai, Zaire.

the half-dozen full-member MSF sections – Spain, Holland, Luxembourg, Belgium, France, and Switzerland. As early as 1988, as one of the founding members of the Canadian MSF recalled their first organizing meetings, "we had a clear vision of a separate Canadian operational section that would have its own style, and its own distinctive Canadian operations." But international MSF is a *European* organization, and its members jealously guard their domain, especially against any hint of an American takeover. At the November 1996 conference in Toronto, when a Canadian MSF bureaucrat casually ventured the opinion that Canadian MSF should "be more independent," an observer from head office in Amsterdam jumped on his comment and suspiciously asked, "What *exactly* do you mean by 'independence'?"

The Degradation of the Market

The commendable effort to be utterly independent from all others, to remain at arm's length from meddlesome governments pursuing their own political ambitions, ironically makes humanitarian agencies more subservient to their audience, more crassly attuned to manipulating the media and the public. Writing in *The Economist*, the incisive British journalist Richard Dowden noted that the new generation of leaders controlling many aid organizations "is more market-orientated," and its objectives tend to be much more narrowly defined as amassing "the most donations." Inevitably, they degrade themselves in such a process.[25]

The nature of the international aid market is that it is "advertised" in the media during major crises – thus, the ferociously competitive world of agency logos, T-shirts, and flags at every conflagration. These pressures turn most humanitarian emergencies into a succession of photo opportunities and logo-flag waving. The front-line players in this game are the often glamorous press officers, the so-called "catastrophe babes" who, Dowden writes, "are incredibly good at giving professional evaluations of the situation," but whose omnipresence "indicates a hidden motive," too crass and obvious a concern for market share.

Relief at an international disaster is at once an aid agency's only product, its only source of revenue, and its best advertisement. In this way, an aid agency's position in the marketplace is similar to a terrorist organization such as the Irish Republican Army. Here, mass murder is both the terrorists' product and its best generator of funds: the latest well-publicized outrage shows the world that the organization is alive and well, and able to disburse its funds in the way the donors intended. Similarly, the task of a press officer is to ensure that her organization is convincingly displayed at the disaster, and attracts the largest number of purchasers (i.e., donors) of her product. Thus, the misery of victims of famine, flood, war, and plague must be underlined, perhaps even exaggerated, if it is to attract sufficient public attention. Similarly, the superiority of her agency to its rivals must be argued vociferously, preferably on international television, regardless of the truth.

This process is inevitably and profoundly corrupting. Aid agencies are necessarily torn between choosing as press officer someone who will represent their agency with accuracy and discretion – thereby perhaps seeming less urgent, less catastrophic, less attention-grabbing – or someone who will approach the task with sufficient lapel-grabbing hyperbole, someone who will feel comfortable enough with disinformation or no information to seize the attention of the media and public funding. Increasingly, their choice is the latter. For their part, press officers will naturally choose their most photogenic and articulate relief workers to represent the agency in brief interviews. "He's so *convincing* on television," cooed one press officer admiringly of her agency's star medical performer. "People will believe *anything* he says." The implication seems clear: credibility begins to matter more than reality.

Such duplicitous and artful mentalities do not sit well with most MSFers in the field, who sweat in out-of-the-way medical stations assessing tuberculosis in Somalia's desert, walking unarmed into Cambodian or Zairean jungles, working with drug addicts in the back streets of Moscow, doing quietly what has to be done to begin to alleviate human suffering in dozens of countries around the world. Such veterans often sit in stunned silence while they watch the new international careerists elbowing each other for centre stage in front of the cameras and microphones.

Crisis Inflation

To ensure the most effective advertising, it may sometimes even seem necessary to inflate the true scale of a catastrophe. "A sort of macabre auction sets in," writes African Rights critic Alex de Waal, "with each relief agency or journalist out-doing the other in prophecies of apocalypse." This is a setting in which "emotive, exaggerated and simplistic messages drive out reasoned and accurate analyses." Such overstatement was the case with the crises in Ethiopia in 1984, Sudan in 1990, Somalia in 1992, and Rwanda in 1996. Yet if there is no apparent limit to the media's appetite for crisis, the media can also be enraged if its sanguine expectations are disappointed. Many media personnel were privately annoyed that aid agencies' predictions of mass death among the Rwandan refugees did not transpire. Of course they did not wish the refugees to die, but they sensed they had been lied to, manipulated by the relief agencies. "We all believed that they were about to die of hunger but this proved to be untrue," one wrote, expressing how the aid agencies had "lost credibility." [26]

Indeed, one journalist concluded that the Rwandan refugee crisis of 1996 might be "a clear example of a case which got too much coverage in relation to what actually occurred. In reality," he thought, "*nothing happened.*" Actually, a great deal happened: hundreds of thousands of refugees returned safely to their homes in Rwanda, and the movement was so well orchestrated that few died en route. In the meantime, out of the way of the cameras in Zaire, tens of thousands of

refugees continued to be shot, tortured, and starved, grop-
ing through the bush for months while they were hunted by
Interhamwe and Zairean militias. When survivors finally
stumbled to safety six months later, MSF commented, many
of the children had bullet or machete wounds. But because it
did not take place in front of the cameras, it did not really
happen. Nevertheless, this should not disguise another reality
– that as is now customary, the "crisis" had been oversold.

"Relief organizations play an angel role as those who save
people in the most terrible places, but they should take care
that the bubble doesn't burst," a European journalist warns.
While this is quite true, aid agencies have no better scientific
means than anyone else to predict the precise dimensions of
an imminent catastrophe. They will surely be chastised if they
underestimate the scale of coming suffering, yet they are
widely seen as "cheating" if the fatalities do not materialize. It
is not a comfortable position.[27]

Does Aid "Do Any Good"?

Alex de Waal has made it clear that while "aid can save lives,"
it "can only mitigate the awfulness and not stop it." Aid is not
"the main factor in determining how many people survive" a
political or ecological crisis: in fact, his best guess is that the
most it can hope for "is to cut mortality rates in half." That
would be a substantial achievement on its own, but aid's

ability to do that is further compromised by backstage political manoeuvres. In Rwanda in 1994, for example, France "promised to save hundreds of thousands, if not millions from genocide and disease," but its self-serving imperial policies "in fact protected at most 14,000 people," many of whom were the *genocidaires*.

Moreover, it was "the natural immunity of the population," not the humanitarian intervention, that spared the refugees the catastrophic spread of disease. Indeed, de Waal writes, "the best news from Africa is that Africans" are adept at surviving their own crises.

> "The worst news is that as happened in Rwanda in 1994, it was a terrible blunder to rush in without a good political assessment and set up huge camps, which became the extremists' bases, protected by the camps' civilian population and fed by what is euphemistically called 'diversion' of humanitarian aid. Sale of surplus aid helped to finance arms-buying sprees. A good proportion of $2 billion in foreign aid enabled a clique of genocidal maniacs to remain in business and begin their killing again, albeit more slowly this time."

Thus, de Waal concludes with his customary acuity, "as in Europe in the 1940s, guns, grenades and genocidal ideology are the main instruments of death in central Africa today, not hunger and disease." To be effective, aid must be based on a cautious political analysis of the situation, so that "a balance can be struck between the charitable imperative and the need to seek political solutions."[28]

MSF **Intellectuals Respond**

MSFers are much given to self-criticism, and struggle to make rational assessments of a situation. No one is more aware than they that aid often does not do what it claims to do; that much aid is wasted and misdirected; and that the provision of aid permits wealthy governments to give the impression that something is being done to help those in crisis. MSFers understand well that the problems they face are not natural, but political – stemming from neglect, corruption, imperial exploitation and machination.

In an MSF hospital near the Burundi border, around a luxurious meal of goat and wet rice to honour our visit, two MSF doctors and an Italian nurse consider the contradictions in their mission. As Carmen tells us: We don't really even understand the impact we have on these people. We come here with our European notions of how to avoid cholera, typhoid, dysentery, and we say, "The water you drink carries things that make you sick and kill you and your children, so you must boil your water before drinking it." But if they are to boil the water, then they must spend much more time gathering wood to make the fires – and this is critical time that every member of the family must normally devote to growing their meagre crops on their tiny plots. So now they have clean water, but not enough food to eat; now they will die not of cholera but of starvation. The same is true if you say, "Your children must be educated." The hours they spend in the village school are deducted from the hours they would otherwise spend in the fields, so in order to escape from the village through education they must starve the village, kill it in order to save it, like the U.S. army in Vietnam. So in the end our work here is neither more useful nor productive in a narrow sense than it would be in Europe or America: quite the contrary, it can be most *harmful*.*

Moreover, adds Georg, we create a lot of ill-feeling in trying to help. We come to these corners of the Third World with many resources, with medicines, food and water, and medical equipment; although increasingly even that is not enough because resistance to antibiotics is increasing here, too, and the classical drug regime is no longer working. But in any case, these things are not self-supporting: they can't afford to buy these things themselves, so when we leave, the resource is gone with us. We only have a short-term positive effect. And what we leave behind – aside from a few people whose lives have been temporarily saved or enriched – is a new and profound sense of frustration. Now they know there is another, richer and safer life, but it is a life they themselves can never lead on their own in their poor and ravaged countries,

---

* Conversations in the remainder of this chapter are a mixture of quotation and paraphrase.

so we leave behind us envy and rage and frustration. If we are lucky, we have amputated enough limbs and sutured enough tendons from machete-severed hands to save a few lives, and taught them simple, attainable hygiene – perhaps to wash their hands after they defecate.

Even in a camp for suspected cholera victims, Georg emphasizes, we have to fight the local governments whose primary concerns are military security and saving money. And these local governments are forever changing their policies. For example, right now in order to keep the refugees moving, the government insists that no one can stay in this camp for more than twenty-four hours, which makes it harder for us to screen the patients and detect diarrhea or cholera, and easier to accidentally release them back into the civilian population where they can spread their diseases. So we can only fight it by fudging how long someone is staying in the camp and spraying everything and everybody down with chlorine to kill the disease. But as soon as they are released and sent home it starts all over again.

With that despairing comment, our lunch in Butare and our fieldwork in Rwanda are finished. We take our leave and head back to Kigali, Bonnie yelping in fear each time our driver races close to a refugee or a cliff edge.

⤶

At the East African headquarters of MSF (Holland) in Nairobi, the darkly handsome administrator, Morris, writhes as he reviews the contradictions in his own work. If we in MSF wish to remain one of the world's major international presences, helping people survive crisis with a measure of dignity, Morris explains, then we have to take part in the degrading public relations–fuelled fight for media recognition. The only way to get funding from a public that gets all its information from television is for the aid agencies to compete with one another for this exposure. And it's sometimes the young and untried agencies that can take the biggest risks and reap the biggest "rewards" in media attention, despite the fact that nothing necessarily is accomplished at all. For example, when the British "New Age Travellers" with their purple Mohawk haircuts drove truckloads of supplies to the former Yugoslavia, they made an enormous splash in the media. Yet 99 per cent of their convoys did not actually get through to their intended targets, and their trucks and supplies ended up in the hands of the enemy military. Still, their extravagant style and ambitions captured media attention and generated visibility and funding.

One of the ten thousand conflicts we are caught in, says Morris, is that people expect the wrong things from aid agencies. They somehow imagine that we can stop wars, but only profound social and economic change – and usually military intervention, at that – can end a war. And the public asks the wrong question: Why should we bother to help when the war will continue to rage? But the whole ethos behind the formation of the Red Cross and the other worthwhile organizations was *to ameliorate* some of the suffering caused by war, not some preposterous pretensions about actually ending the war. They also ask if humanitarian aid sometimes prolongs a war; and I am sure it does, but it is a reasonable and humane goal to make a war more fair, less cruel. It's not necessarily bad, for example, to prolong a war if there is less starvation and suffering and torture of civilians. The *right questions* are: Can and does humanitarian aid do any good? And if so, for whom? This is what our most thoughtful critics such as Alex de Waal ask.

Morris says the thoughtless ask, "Why don't we just let them fight it out and kill each other off if that's what they want to do?" But we wouldn't be working for MSF if we believed that, if we could turn our backs in this way on human anguish of such magnitude – and remember, it is always the innocent people with no political axe to grind who are the victims, never the *genocidaires*. We have to do what we can to encourage governments to work for a politics of reconciliation between warring parties: we can do nothing else, since we in MSF are apolitical and without such power.

Morris emphasizes that one of the many problems in dealing with the media is that so few television people have a sense of history or any awareness of what goes on in the modern world, and all they are really looking for is a media-worthy event – to bring in their stars to stand on the road for ten minutes surrounded by misery. The genocide and the refugee crisis that followed in Rwanda is a good illustration: it captured world attention because by its very nature it was Good Television, all those refugees pounding up a narrow road, it fits in the cameras! But why is something special being made of the genocide of the Tutsis, as if such a holocaust were in any way unusual in this world? Why is it different in any way from all those genocides perpetrated in the last decade by Bokassa in the Central African Empire, Mengistu in Ethiopia, and Amin in Uganda – genocides that were impossible to televise and therefore didn't really happen? How is it different in any way from what befell the refugees who fled to Zaire after the genocide to live without food on lava rock; dying in their thousands from cholera and rape, machete and bullet from various "rebels" and militias? It's just that the media had access to Rwanda, and the Cold War was over, so the catastrophe could get the "sympathy" of the First World. But in getting the sympathy, it completely denies the near universality of the experience in the Third World.

We aid agencies, Morris continues, are often criticized for actually prolonging wars, and in an important sense our critics are right. Just by being there, MSF and others add legitimacy to the warlord and his faction – it appears as if we are ambassadors from the First World to his court. Moreover, what we don't give them, they will steal from us; and in either case we're making both the warlord's army and his refugees less war-weary, we're refreshing them so they can continue the war. We are also making it possible for the local warlords to keep their useful civilians alive – not that most of them care at all about their populations – because they know we'll do it for them, so their energies are freed to make more savage and prolonged war. No one has come up with an answer to this.

We can't be expected to start making political distinctions between those we will help and those we will not, we can't be expected to say, "We save Tories but not Liberals." We are a humanitarian organization. Let the politicians resolve the political problem.

Morris observes that the aid agencies are always blamed for failing somehow to "fix" the situation, but it is *politics* that makes it last longer. And it's money that the warlords are competing for – in "foreign aid" from the First World, and in the exploitation of the natural resources and people of a country. In Zaire and Liberia, for example, there is vast wealth in the diamonds, the gold, and the timber. Humanitarian aid is just the media-friendly initiative from the First World, but legal, political, and economic intervention are all required if anything is going to be solved. If there had been any serious attention paid in the first place to real social, economic, and political development and the elimination of inequalities, the wars would never have started. Zaire has been crumbling for years, its dictator supported (for their own self-serving reasons) by the corrupt security services of the U.S., France, and Belgium. Yet when it blows up, all they do is throw in humanitarian aid.

Pausing briefly to sip his now-cold coffee, Morris continues: One of the jobs of humanitarian aid is to provide assistance to people who are hurt by war, but inevitably you get involved in the political process as an advocate to make war more fair. It may be longer, but it can be better. What are the real consequences of a war for the people? One of our worst

On the road in southern Rwanda.

dilemmas is that we legitimize warlords just by being there, by establishing a temporary hospital among the refugees a warlord uses as his human shield. We give the warlord official status. But the levels of human-rights abuse are terrible, and *witnessing* – observing the evil that they do and telling the world – is one of our primary responsibilities. Witnessing is why MSF was founded. It's not just moralizing, either: leaders are less unlikely to comply with international rules when witnesses are there. For example, when the refugees from Sierra Leone in Liberia were lying in their beds in hospital, starving and fearful, waiting to be robbed, raped, and murdered by the soldiers, MSF witnessing was important to them, I can tell you!

We claim we are apolitical and don't take sides, Morris admits. But not all forms of neutrality are productive. Our gut feeling is that witnessing is of fundamental importance – not that MSF is always the first or the only witness. Often people don't want us in their region because they know we'll talk about what we see: starvation, or the routine kidnapping of refugees to use as hostages. We've often been thrown out of countries for our "crimes," as when we protested the massive deportations of civilians and the dumping of whole populations in Mengistu's Ethiopia. We try to do everything from just hanging around the warlord to let him know we know what he's doing to his people, to calling in the UN, to alerting the world's news agencies. Believe it or not, there were so many MSF and other relief-agency witnesses in Bosnia that the worst of the abuses were curtailed. Many of our ethnic Dinka nurses in the Sudan were slaughtered by the government in 1993 for the crime of cooperating with us, but the survivors are still there; and aid agencies play a real role in developing a local sense of civic and social responsibility.

Another common and legitimate criticism of aid agencies is that since they are often government financed and therefore dependent, the government takes control and uses the aid agencies as an instrument for their own political agenda. This is often quite true and has to be watched at all times, and it is why MSF struggles to keep its distance from government. Many see relief as just a business, another bureaucratic career strategy for the middle classes, but that's simplistic conspiracy theory. It's true for some, but there are many agencies that don't pay at all: I get twelve thousand a year for running all the services in this entire country.

Morris concludes with the observation that Africa Watch's Alex de Waal, aid's most gifted critic, has often admitted he was mystified why so many people of such intelligence work for these agencies. MSF was formed by intellectuals *to make direct action*, not to sit around asking questions. And it's a good thing, since we're the only people who can act fast: while the UN sits on its hands as it always does, we're already in there doing what we can. We've made lots of mistakes, but what is the alternative? To let the Rwandan genocide happen in 1994 and just sit and do nothing? We're gravely handicapped, it is true: you don't know the language, the culture, the politics, you go in and try to help; you make mistakes, but you cannot do nothing, can you? It's better to do something than nothing, of this we are absolutely sure. The world economy can afford a humanitarian ideal.

〜

In the MSF (France) headquarters in the heart of Nairobi, pale and chain-smoking French MSF intellectuals gather daily in their dank and musky basement "think-tank" to debate and assess their direct actions. Unlike MSF (Belgium), which is 90 per cent government financed, MSF (France) receives 60 per cent of its financing from private donors. This gives it a relative freedom from political intervention – although it is sometimes accused of spying for its government – and it tightly resists any attempts to control its actions. Three French MSFers share their morning with us.

Our aim, says Eric through a cloud of tobacco smoke, is to analyse the contradictions resulting from our work – as in how we are prolonging the war by giving assistance, or how we are offering an alibi for the international community, an excuse to do nothing. We witness a lot of the side effects. For example, since the end of the Cold War, international power groups are involving themselves in peacekeeping, but in doing so are not coming to the roots of starvation. So we are actually detrimental in a sense, because the international community uses us as an alibi to say "we are doing something," and all we're doing is just giving out food and drugs. That's one problem.

We at MSF are used as a convenient smokescreen to hide the lack of willingness of the international community to intervene. There is no real interest in intervention. They don't want to risk offending public opinion in their own country by losing soldiers, and they just want to give that public the impression they are doing something to satisfy public concern. No country wants to risk its soldiers dying for a country nobody cares about. But they can say, "Look, we have MSF in there, we have the Red Cross and the UN in there, we're doing the best we can."

This especially reveals itself in Rwanda, Eric asserts, stopping to suck his cigarette. In 1994, MSF waged an international campaign to make people understand that genocide is not a humanitarian crisis, it's a *political* crisis. We cannot stop a genocide by humanitarian action, we need military action to stop armed killers. Instead of listening to us, the international community did nothing. Later, when the television was full of refugees, they decided to give aid, but the evil was already done, the million were dead! In 1994, military intervention in Rwanda should have taken the form of a "security zone" – a refugee area with heavy military protection – to provide non-combatants with safe havens where they could escape harassment, rape, and murder.

The idea of security zones has been spoiled by the disaster in Yugoslavia; where a zone was created but nothing was done to secure it and protect the population. In fact, however, a security zone is the only thing that can work to save lives in the midst of "ethnic cleansing." For example, during the recent Liberian civil war that MSF was so heavily involved in, the Community of West African States decided to establish a security zone, but it was run by the Nigerians who were pursuing their own political aims in Liberia. Every country has its own agenda: security zones are a good idea, but politics destroy it unless rigorous contrary steps are taken. If only the UN worked properly; if it had any teeth; if it was not in the control of the States and its imperial aims. The only way a security zone can work is if the country in charge of a UN military force has *no* agenda, or an agenda that is consistent with humanitarian concerns. This happened in Kurdistan in the wake of the Gulf War, and if the idea is followed properly, we believe such a system would work.

To begin with, an international principle must be established at the International Court in Geneva that defines refugees as an international problem, Eric suggests. The problem at the moment is that if people do not cross a border, they do not have refugee status, and there is no legal obligation of any kind to help them. Now governments are trying to stop refugees from crossing borders for just that reason, and a prime task of the UN must be to facilitate the flight of refugees.

We in MSF are used by the warring factions in so many ways. In Liberia, the factions in the civil war tried to manipulate us by giving us so little information about the country that we put our assistance where they wanted it, not necessarily where it was needed. Moreover, they manipulate the security environment by making unsafe any areas where they don't want us, that is, where their enemies might be helped. They want assistance to the area they control – so if you try to assist the other side, they will attack you. Again, they consciously use the victims of the struggle – the refugees – exhibiting them when they know there will be intervention from us. They create needs: they will purposely starve their populations so that malnutrition rates increase dramatically within weeks and they can say to us, "Look, there is a lot of need here. You must set up a general program of aid." If you bring them food, you are encouraging their strategy – aha, it works! – and if you don't, their captive populations will die. If you denounce it, you will be expelled – and you then take the risk of not being active any more. It's a very cruel dilemma. They ask aid agencies to pay "taxes," they overestimate the numbers of people affected to get more food and supplies, they force you to keep an armed escort and you must pay for the guards, and so on.

These strategies for the factions are clever attempts to fuel their economy, but there are also plenty of resources they could sell under the table: timber, iron ore, and diamonds are of far greater economic value than any of our aid. So, the real purpose of what they are doing is to control their population with food and medicine, and *to get political legitimacy* by having a population under their control. At the same time, they can also use the population as slaves, as they did in Liberia – it is not the fighters who dig the mines or cut the timber. They are also used as a human shield – these militias seldom attack each other, but attack their rival's unarmed civilian population.

Eric lights another cigarette. Still, if you want your agency to be in there helping, you must deal with a warlord. But in doing so, you recognize him as the authority. It is a form of diplomatic representation. They can say, "Look, on my turf I have MSF, Red Cross, UNHRC. I am recognized. Maybe there is no diplomatic representative, but there are NGOs [nongovernmental organizations], so we have *de facto* international recognition." It's also a good way to attract the attention of the media. So the status of aid agencies is by no means clear: Are they private or public actors? Are they representing a foreign state? They also provide good propaganda when the other side attacks your civilians – and the warlord finds it easy to say, "Look, the other side are barbarians."

It's hard for MSF. On the one hand, the international community is playing with one or other of the warring parties. We try to explain to the world what is happening. We are always asking ourselves if we are doing right or wrong. Would it be any better without us? At the same time, people are dying and you cannot do nothing.

It is a very cruel dilemma. But there are so many dilemmas. Take the South Sudan project, an emergency program for the flood victims, forty-five thousand of whom lost everything, including their land and homes. One of our constraints right now is our own French government's agenda in the Sudan – France is the *only* western country that supports Khartoum. Now France has supplied satellite photographs of the Sudanese rebels so they can be attacked by Khartoum's forces. It is not clear why France is doing this, but the rebels now see us as spies for the French government. Indeed, in 1994, two MSFers were taken hostage and accused of being spies, caught in an area where the best satellite photographs had been supplied. MSF (France) was then thrown out of the Sudan, and when we come back, we have to be clandestine, supplying seeds for the crops to prevent starvation and disease, and let MSFers from other countries deal with the cholera, tuberculosis, and malaria epidemics that decimate people who have no food or medical care.

"Why are we in the Sudan?" Marcel interrupts. "The Sudan is a very difficult situation for MSF – two of us were killed there – but MSF's history with the Sudan is a love story. We want to be part of it, an effective dimension: maybe it is linked to the tragic past. It is very easy to fall in love with these people," he adds.

"Yes, when they meet you they form a bond with you that you don't want to break, and when you leave you don't want anything to happen to them," an American nurse working for MSF (Switzerland) concludes. "But at the same time you have to use your head. Some programs are very expensive but still do not address the most vital needs of the population. What is our purpose? Ultimately, perhaps the most important thing the aid agencies do is keep the situation from completely exploding."

6

The Ecstasy of Moral Clarity

"The world can afford a humanitarian ideal."
— MSF country manager

What is the point of MSF? It cannot possibly help all those in need; indeed, it cannot even offer aid to the majority. Moreover, what help it can provide is often negated by the ugly reality that many of its patients will later be murdered by the warlords, or die from hunger, disease, or AIDS.

It is indeed caught in a terrible and cruel dilemma. There is no way for it to be certain that its decisions are the right ones: only time and leisurely analysis can reveal that, and these are luxuries MSF does not have. MSF emergency response teams can only do what they understand the best – rapidly assess a situation and act immediately. Yet in acting quickly,

Opposite: Emergency way station on refugee route, Rwanda.

mistakes are made, resources squandered: that is the price that must be paid.

The point of MSF has nothing to do with whether it can save the world – it cannot possibly hope to do so. Its social legitimacy can perhaps be best understood through an analogy with the philosophy that precipitated the abolition of capital punishment throughout the civilized western world. That philosophy did not capture the imagination of the world because it stated that kidnappers and murderers had any claim to humanity, or even any right to live. Rather, it did so as a solemn declaration that *there has been enough killing*. Thus, the state protects the tawdry life of a killer not out of respect for his person, but to maintain a social principle – that the state has no more right to take a life than does any individual. In this way, the doctrine of the sanctity of life can universally be maintained.

The work of MSF is a similar declaration that we struggle to be civilized. The world can afford a humanitarian ideal, and it cannot afford the brutalization that comes with indifference to catastrophe. However powerful the wish may be to deny it, each nation is part of this planet; and each political, cultural, and economic act reverberates throughout the world. Moreover, MSF is relatively cheap. These are no bloated careerist bureaucrats: they sleep on foam mats and eat a meal or two a day, they live only for their work and save little or nothing, they bring credit to our tainted civilization and its grievous history of world war, brutal imperialism, and mass extermination.

MSFers are often seen as the reckless "cowboys" of the international aid movement because they help first and ask questions later. Indeed, their occasionally shrill and sanctimonious style makes many enemies. Yet if they see their action has been inappropriate or misguided, they will reverse their decisions. They are not gripped by that bureaucratic paralysis that makes the United Nations so universally despised – perching ineffectually in the best hotels and restaurants, their thumbs in their collective fundament, as a genocide or plague unfolds. When MSF sees hunger, disease, or mass murder, they witness it for the world, and they do whatever they can to assuage it.

They do not retreat in fearful impotence as does so much of the international community. Many of the Rwandans who were slaughtered in the spring of 1994 remained in the capital city despite the obvious danger, because they had a tragically misplaced confidence in the UN. When Human Rights Watch/ Africa later asked the few survivors why they had remained when they might have fled to safety, "they replied that they had not been able to imagine the UN troops standing by while Rwandans were massacred." In fact, it took the UN six months to redeploy after it had pulled its tiny, underarmed, and ineffectual force out of the country; six months during which the genocide was completed; six months for member nations to haggle with one another to maximize the political profit they might reap from the venture. Near the end of the extermination, *one* UN monitor was actually placed in Rwanda, but "she remained alone for two months, a single person to attempt to discourage and investigate abuses for a population of some five million people. Until late August, she had no vehicle, no communications equipment and no computer."[29]

MSF has a knack for stepping on the toes of others in the aid industry, and it jeers unmercifully at the aid circus's parade of leather-lined and air-conditioned luxury four-wheel-drives ferrying the recipients of preposterous European salaries from luxury hotel to expensive restaurant. Neither is MSF there to deliver some coercive mandate, demanding religious or political conversion in return for western food and medicine – as a century of missionaries and imperial rivals have done and continue to do. Nor is it there to further the political aims of some rancid political power, anxious to consolidate or enlarge its domain. Certainly MSFers are not there for crude, self-serving reasons: their ascetic style – a few hundred dollars a month plus room and board, sleeping in tents or rented rooms, eating where and what they can – lies largely outside the careerist syndrome. Their ecstatic fulfilment comes instead from what they do, and what the doing does to them, and for us.

The twentieth century's enthusiastic participation in the twin apocalypses of world war and genocide destroyed what simple faith western civilization had in its morality and its heroes. What can there be left to believe in after reading the Nazis' instructions to their killing squads in Eastern Europe, reminding them that when machine-gunning groups of villagers, it is essential to aim low enough to ensure the children

are hit? In the modern world, only fools – religious funda-
mentalists, demagogues of all stripes, the naïve, and the uned-
ucated – still proclaim that there is such a thing as honour in
public or private affairs.

Indeed, in the great literature of our time the protagonist
has come to be an *anti*-hero, one who by definition lacks
the admirable attributes of nobility of mind and spirit, a life
marked by action or purpose. Our new hero is a kind of
depressed failure, and the essence of his being is anguish, self-
doubt, and distrust of society. Symptomatic of our mentality,
the novelist Graham Greene, in *A Burnt-Out Case*, used a
sycophantic charlatan to romanticize the motives of Querry, a
jaded and heartsick European working in a leper colony in
Zaire: "You want to know what makes him [Querry] tick? I
am sure that it is love, a completely selfless love without the
barrier of colour or class."[30]

The distrust is so deeply rooted that should a Dr. Albert
Schweitzer expend his substance in some African bush hospital, or a Mother Teresa devote her life tending to the poor of
Calcutta, an industry will surely be created to damage their
repute. As soon as they become cultural icons, a counter-
attack will be mounted: now it will be "discovered" that their
methods and goals are authoritarian, even ethnocentric and
eccentric, and therefore worthless. Should people devote
their lives to caring for the children of the poor, it may even
be hinted, or assumed, or expected, that they are also pedo-
philes abusing their charges. Such is the spirit of the times, as
enervating as the corruption it exposes.

Indeed, it sometimes appears as if the media assume that everyone lies, and nothing is as it appears to be. Under the headline "PHOTOS THAT LIE," the Canadian journal of record reminds us that "some famous historical shots" were fakes, and asks with ill-concealed delight: "Remember that famous photo of the sailor dipping the nurse on VJ Day? It was posed. Ditto the equally renowned shot of two lovers kissing in a Paris street. The raising of the flag at Iwo Jima did happen, but not the way it was pictured. The Marines had already put up a flag, but raised a second, bigger one because they thought it would look better. Now, be truthful. Are you disappointed?"[31]

This focused cynicism is as it should be, for if the world runs on fear and greed, much of it is built on a tissue of lies. Indeed, too few perceive the ethical wilderness that shapes their lives. There is, however, a truth too often concealed in modern commentary – and it is concealed somewhere between the ancient and nonsensical claims that supermen advanced to save the world on behalf of Christianity and Civilization, and the equally noxious assumption that since humans are profoundly flawed they must all therefore be utterly corrupt. In some persons and institutions, there can be a congruence between self-serving desires and the needs of suffering humanity. Perhaps a craving for adventure, a need for a legitimizing sense of accomplishment, a dash of moral superiority, an ascetic sense of self-denial, can have positive consequences?

When the rapes and massacres, the plagues, the famines, the floods, or the droughts erupt anywhere in the world, the world stands still. MSF does not. It can place its emergency medical teams and equipment anywhere in the world within twenty-four hours. In the opinion of one thoughtful Third World medical practitioner, MSF's genius is that "they are 'smoke jumpers,' and their job is putting out fires rather than preventing them. In times of disaster, the big divisions are slow moving up into the line, but MSF can get there in time to give first aid when it counts."

In the crisis zone, MSFers act as if they do not care that they are taking terrible risks; or that in helping one they may unintentionally assist another who is less deserving; or whether aid is or is not "a good investment." They go about their business with that single-minded energy that accompanies a clear sense of purpose. It is what they know how to do; it is worth doing; and they do it better than almost anyone else.

Working for MSF liberates them as human beings, freeing them from the triviality of personal woes and the mindlessness of modern life. Focusing utterly on their acts, they give witness to the abominations in the world and treat its survivors. They dig the latrines, they ferry pure water, they treat the mutilated, the starved, and the pestilent. They make few distinctions between the innocent and the guilty and so perform a kind of righteous penance for the machinations of racist imperialism. In acting thus, their personal dilemmas dissolve and their identities fuse. Through their healing gifts of medicine and emotional connection, they achieve a kind of heart-pounding ecstasy.

Writing from Zaire, an M.D. describes his life and his beloved MSF: "An approaching war. Machine guns, military, mercenaries and rebels. In the middle of nowhere 150,000 refugees from Rwanda create a camp on the road in a village named Tingi Tingi. Out of guilt, out of fear, out of collective hysteria, they fled the rebels' attack on their previous camp near Bukavu and headed west instead of east. They walked 500 km through the forest, their feet mangled, eating roots and stems and now they are here. I spend several hours a day rounding on the most severe cases. In a tent, on the ground, in the mud of the rainy season, 30 starving children and their desperate mothers. Nasogastric tubes to force feed the feeble. IV lines and injections to fight bacterial fires and the shock of diarrheal dehydration. The ubiquitous red plastic mugs and plates of feeding centres. Déjà vu. They stare at you, these little ones with bodies like frogs and little monkeys. No flesh. They never smile. And when you return later, several have gone. Without a whisper."[32]

⤸

Late one night in December 1996, in Nairobi airport's departure lounge, we prepare to quit Africa and MSF for good. The three of us sit across the aisle from a breathtakingly beautiful woman: she has an utterly serene face and confidently makes direct and fearless eye contact. We notice the MSF stickers on each other's hand luggage, and she tells us she has spent six years in medical work with MSF – mostly in Sierra Leone, but this last month in Rwanda's emergency. She is going home to the Netherlands for a visit: she has not been with her family for the last eight Christmases, and in any case she needs a break from her beloved Africa. "I love Holland, too, but it is hard to leave your friendships here," she explains. We wish each other good luck getting on the plane in Kenya, and then again the following morning when disembarking in Amsterdam. She has the regal air of someone at peace with herself and in charge of her own life.

The hardest thing is not to arrive, but to leave MSF. When you leave, you lose all contact with the centre of the world, with one another, with the suffering, and with yourself. You are out of the loop, no longer part of the sweaty action or the gripping flow of news. Now you will be deprived of the brief romances and the warm friendships that come from sharing so much tension, deprivation, and hard work. Suddenly, and cruelly, all the loving arms and comforting cheeks will be torn from your shoulders and your life. If you are lucky, you may get a Christmas card – perhaps to memorialize this double death that is the loss of intimacy and the reacquisition of conventional life. No wonder they return again and again, these MSFers.

⤺

For our part, we merely sense that we have been jettisoned, like empty canisters. Once home in Newfoundland, we are informed that MSF maintains a sophisticated psychological support team for those who have returned from the field. "Call collect, at any time you feel the need," they tell us. One month later, sensing that some terrible Rwandan wound has opened in my soul, I decide to ask them for help. Following their instructions, I call collect. The husband of the physician who runs the support team answers the telephone and I identify myself. "Elliott somebody?" I hear him saying to another man. "Never heard of him." He refuses the call and abruptly hangs up. The grating buzz of the disconnected line underscores this new emptiness, and reminds us that we are alone again.

Appendix: MSF Operations

In 1995, MSF International had as many as three thousand volunteers working in Afghanistan, China/Tibet, Sri Lanka, Bangladesh, Burma, Cambodia, Thailand, Vietnam, Hong Kong, Laos, Philippines, the Russian Federation, Armenia and Azerbaijan, Tajikistan, Georgia, the former Yugoslavia, Albania, Romania, Israel/The Palestinian Authority, Lebanon, Yemen, Zaire, Rwanda, Burundi, Tanzania, Djibouti, Ethiopia, Somalia, Kenya, Uganda, Sudan, Liberia, Sierra Leone, Guinea, Ivory Coast, Equatorial Guinea, Mali, Mauritania, Chad, Angola, Madagascar, Malawi, Mozambique, South Africa, Zimbabwe, Bolivia, Brazil, Colombia, Peru, Cuba, Haiti, Panama, Nicaragua, Guatemala, Mexico, as well as with vulnerable populations in Belgium, France, and Spain.

Missions are launched in areas disrupted by war, massive population movements, famine, and natural or social disasters. When MSF learns of a developing crisis, it immediately sends an inspection team to assess the situation. A coordinating

MSF doctor conducts test for Kala-Azar in her bathroom.

task force will then decide whether conditions warrant further involvement, and volunteers and equipment will be dispatched within hours to the troubled zone. Once there, MSF accepts responsibility for a range of emergency medical interventions that include the provision of basic health care, the construction of water and sanitation facilities, the provision of supplementary foodstuffs to vulnerable groups, the training of local health workers, as well as the control and prevention of epidemics.

Since the founding of the Canadian office in 1991, 181 Canadians have worked abroad with MSF. In 1995, MSF Canada's income was close to $2.5 million, $1.5 million of which came from the Canadian International Development Agency (CIDA) and $500,000 from MSF (Holland). In addition, well over $200,000 came from private donations and various promotions.

For information, contact the Doctors Without Borders Canadian office at

355 Adelaide St. W., 5B
Toronto, Ontario
M5V 1S2
Tel: (416) 586-9820
Fax: (416) 586-9821

Notes

1. All personal names have been disguised, and all quotations are as precise as can be made while scribbling in the back of lurching Land Cruisers or under the arc of artillery fire.

2. Radio Mille Collines, Rwanda, quoted in Fergal Keane, *Season of Blood: A Rwandan Journey* (New York: Viking, 1995), p. vii.

3. Alan Zarembo, "Hutu Killer Feels Safer in Jail," *Globe and Mail*, December 13, 1996; Zarembo, *The Economist*, December 7, 1996, pp. 42–43.

4. Pierre Clastres, *Archaeology of Violence* (New York: Semiotext(e), 1984), p. 183.

5. Arnold Toynbee, *Experiences* (London: Oxford University Press, 1969), pp. 241–242.

6. Zygmunt Bauman, *Modernity and the Holocaust* (Oxford: Polity Press, 1989), pp. 91, 122.

7. See David Fromkin, *A Peace To End All Peace: The Fall of the Ottoman Empire and the Creation of the Modern Middle East* (New York: Avon, 1989); Leo Kuper, *Genocide: Its Political Use in the Twentieth Century* (New Haven: Yale University Press, 1982), pp. 115–116.

8. Despite the Armenians' success in Turkish commercial and intellectual life, an estimated 80 per cent of them were peasants. See Kuper, p. 116.

9. *Proceedings of Nuremberg*, quoted in Kuper, p. 43.

10. For a discussion of how close even a pacific society can come to genocidal behaviour in special circumstances, see the extraordinary analysis of Norwegian guards in Nazi concentration camps in Nils Christie's marvellous *Crime Control As Industry: Towards GULAGS, Western Style?* (New York: Routledge, 1993). From Kuper, p. 55. See also Bauman.

11. Scott Anderson, "Prisoner of War," *Harper's*, January 1997, pp. 35–54. See press reports for Interhamwe's tactics.

12. Keane, p. 22. Approximately the size of Maryland, Rwanda has a population density of four hundred per square kilometre. Gerard Prunier, *The Rwanda Crisis: History of a Genocide* (New York: Columbia University Press, 1995); Francois Jean (ed.), *Populations in Danger 1995* (London: Médecins Sans Frontières, 1995), pp. 30–31.

13. Bertrand Russell, quoted in Keane, pp. 12–13, 16–21, 23–24, 26–30. See also press reports, and MSF publications such as *World in Crisis: The Politics of Survival at the End of the 20th Century*, 1997.

14. James C. McKinley, Jr., reprinted in *The East African*, November 11–17, 1996.

15. I am especially grateful here to Mon Vanderostyne for generously sharing with us both his passion and his unsparing critical intelligence.

16. Days after the massacres, the sites were visited by anthropologist Dorothy Anger. Her CBC Radio report, "Rwanda Maps," deserves to be heard.

17. Bruce Wallace, "The Trouble With Aid," *Maclean's*, December 16, 1996, pp. 34–37.

18. Eric Wolf, *Peasant Wars of the 20th Century* (New York: Harper, 1973), p. 280.

19. John Berger and Jean Mohr, *A Seventh Man: A Book of Images and Words About the Experience of Migrant Workers in Europe* (London: Penguin, 1975).

20. Anderson, pp. 35–54.

21. Barbara Ehrenreich, "The Women Who Heal," in Rick Smolan, Phillip Moffitt, and Matthew Naythons (eds.), *The Power To Heal: Ancient Arts and Modern Medicine* (New York: Prentice Hall, 1990), pp. 84–86.

22. From Médecins Sans Frontières' *Clinical Guidelines: Diagnostic and Treatment Manual* (Paris: Hatier, 1990).

23. Greg Locke, "Field Notes," 1996.

24. Robert D. Kaplan, *The Ends of the Earth: A Journey at the Dawn of the 21st Century* (New York: Random House, 1996), pp. 432–433.

25. Richard Dowden, quoted in *Information*, January 3, 1997, Denmark.

26. Alex de Waal, "Crisis for Christmas," *The Spectator*, November 16, 1996, p. 26; *Information*, January 3, 1997.

27. Niels Carstensen and Richard Dowden, quoted in *Information*, January 3, 1997.

28. Alex de Waal, "Why One Million Will Not Die," *Prospect*, December 1996, pp. 76–77. And "Crisis for Christmas," *The Spectator*, November 16, 1996, pp. 26–27. De Waal is co-director of the London-based human rights organization Africa Rights.

29. *Human Rights Watch/Africa*, December 1994, vol. 6, no. 12, p. 13.

30. Graham Greene, *A Burnt-Out Case* (New York: Penguin, 1963), p. 134.

31. *Globe and Mail*, November 9, 1996.

32. Milton Tectonidis, in *MSF Dispatches*, Spring/Summer 1997, p. 6.

Index